A SHORT HISTORY OF IRELAND

SEAN McMAHON

MERCIER PRESS

For Marie and Frank D'Arcy

Mercier Press
PO Box 5 5 French Church Street Cork
16 Hume Street Dublin 2

First published 1996
© Sean McMahon 1996
A CIP record for this book is available from the British Library.
ISBN 1 85635 137 8
10 9 8 7 6 5

Cover painting: 'The Dublin Volunteers in College Green' by Francis Wheatley courtesy of the National Gallery of Ireland
Cover design by Bluett
Typeset by Richard Parfrey
Printed in Ireland by ColourBooks Baldoyle Dublin 13

CONTENTS

1

THE WINTER ISLAND

It was Gaius Julius Caesar, who on paper at least divided all Gaul into three parts, that first recorded Ireland's name as 'Hibernia' – the winter place. His two hurried visits across the English Channel in 55 and 54 BC did no more than establish a domain of interest; the conquest of Britain and southern Scotland was left to Claudius and others. By AD 82 the eagle had established itself as far north as the Solway Firth and County Antrim was less than a day's journey away. The *gubernator Britanniae*, Gnaeus Julius Agricola, was on the point of a narrow sea invasion with ships and armies primed and an Irish princeling ready for imposition, but trouble with the German mercenaries in Galloway or the threat of another attack by the painted Picts from middle or northern Caledonia deflected, postponed and finally caused the abandonment of any Irish adventure.

The wintry land that the Romans disdained had had inhabitants for at least 7,000 years. The earliest people of the period known to palaeontologists as mesolithic (Middle Stone Age) were hunters who had almost certainly followed deer, their main quarry, especially the great elk, across the land bridges that existed before the rise of sea levels that followed the end of the last ice age (*c.* 10,000 BC) established it and its neighbours as islands and no longer part of the main. With the slow increase in temperature, the mosses that were the main vegetation of the tundra lands were transmogrified into hardwood trees which grew in such abundance that the island, except for the wet lands of bog, lake and river marges, became heavily afforested. The great elk died out then, some say because with antlers eight foot wide it could not live in the forest, and the early inhabitants had to subsist on smaller mammals like wild pig and fish and game. They made spears and axes of flint and bone and were nomadic to the extent that they had to follow their food. Archaeological evidence of the existence of these early people has been found at Mount Sandel, near Coleraine in north County Derry, and at Lough Boora in Offaly.

When with the coming of Christianity the Irish at last found a means of making a written record of their early history: the model they used was of a series of invasions going back to the time of Noah's flood. These are almost entirely mythical but they may well reflect a folk memory of actual immigration and assimilation. The oldest document about these early incursionists was the *Lebor Gabála* (*Book of Invasions*) and it lists among others Fomorians, giant sea-pirates who came from the islands of the north, Fir Bolg and Milesians who hailed from Spain. The name Fir Bolg could disguise the Belgae, who probably made their way to the south coast through the English Channel, the Hispanic origins of the sons of Mil could well have been a euhemeristic version of an actual incursion from Iberia and the Fomorian giants may have been a memory of early Scandinavian freebooters.

The Irish Celts were curious not only about about their own past but also about that of their predecessors on the westerly island. They sought explanations for the megalithic remains, dolmens, passage graves and tumuli (especially those which dominated the fertile basin of the Boyne) that they viewed with a religious awe. The special reverence and potency associated with Tara and Emain Macha that persisted into historical times is part of the same process. The word Celts (*Keltoi* to the Greeks and *Celtae* to the Romans) may never have been used by the people themselves. The name was applied to an nomadic and warlike people who, originating in south central Europe, spread east and west. These warriors were equipped with iron weapons and fought battles on foot and from spiked-wheeled chariots. They attacked Delphi and sacked Rome but were just as happy to fight with each other, preferring to maintain small independent tribal units. They fought naked or in linen shirts and relied on individual bravery and noise to try to cow their enemies. Their Irish descendants continued to affect this armourless battle gear even against the invading Normans who were protected by chain mail and had stirruped war horses.

The Celts' fascination with those they perceived as their own particular ancestors seems positively Shintoist. They held in their imaginations a heroic age with epic warriors and conflicts, and queens as powerful and independent as any king. The main question that confronts historians of this quasi-historical period is whether the waves of immigration which archaeologists confirm were actual recurring conquests of the people of the last wave, or merely colonisation of other parts of a fairly empty and heavily wooded land. The Celts have made the greatest impression because their characteristic artefacts, marked by rich and subtle design, are found all over Europe, but they may not have been even the largest group of finally homogeneous people who by the fifth century could be called Gaels and were to be the object of the attention of Christian missionaries. They had by then a common language a version of *ur*-Celtic that finally became Irish, Manx and Gaelic.

In this language they created, memorised and passed down by word of mouth marvellous tales about what they held as their past. The great prose and verse epic *Táin Bó Cuailgne* which tells of an epic struggle between Connacht's Medb and Ulster's Conchubar and describes the death of Cú Chulainn, the greatest of the northern heroes, may have its origin in the struggle which pushed the historical Ulaid east of the Bann. Aesthetics aside, the most significant thing about the epic is that a bull is at its centre. The great Gaels of Ireland, as Chesterton called them, may have been bonny fighters but they were fighting farmers and stockmen. They were almost pathologically independent and isolated each from the other, preferring small divisions of territory with settlements not unlike the ranch system of the early American West. The ringforts which are to be found in great profusion all over the country – about 60,000 in all – and which were called fairy forts in more romantic times, are remains of these homesteads. A hundred feet in diameter, the bank enclosed a circular yard with a dwelling and outhouses. The purpose of the ramp in simple dwellings was mainly as a perimeter mark and a defence against wild boar and wolves. Richer people (wealth measured in terms of cattle) who felt more threatened usually had triple ramparts with deep ditches in between. The grandest and oddest of all the Gaelic dwellings was the *crannóg*, an artificial island built in the middle of a lake reached either by boat or by specially constructed (and disposable) causeway, which only the very rich could afford. The Irish proverb: '*Ar scáth a chéile a mhaireas na daoine*,' belongs to a later social configuration. Those from the parts of the country where the Gaelic system was allowed to persist until Tudor times found towns, created by Ostmen and Normans and English, intolerably claustrophobic and preferred to live as much as possible in the open air.

The social and political unit was the *tuath* and at one period (from the seventh to the eighth century) when the total population of the island was less than half a million, there were up to 200 of these tiny pastoral and agricultural entities. They were ruled by a king (*rí*) whose main purposes were to supervise the *oenach* (local assembly), lead them in battle and act as a focus for quasi-religious respect. The *tuatha* were usually part of a cluster governed by an 'over-king', larger groups which became the basis for the episcopal dioceses which were organised in the twelfth century. These in turn formed themselves into major confederations: the

'Five Fifths of Ireland', Ulaid, Mide, Laigin, Mumha and Connachta. The modern provincial division has Leinster incorporating both Mide and Laigin but the Irish word for province (*cúige*) is a mute reminder that the four provinces of Ireland once were five.

It still seems odd that a country the size of Ireland with a homogeneous social system and a common language should have remained for a millennium so petulantly disunited. From time to time charismatic leaders appeared. The famous Niall Noíghiallach ('Niall of the Nine Hostages') whom the older stories personally implicate in the snatch of Patrick seems to have been a real person. He is taken to have come from Connacht and to have risen to great power because of successful freebooting raids on the west coasts of Scotland and Britain. His direct descendants called themselves the Uí Néill and by the seventh century they dominated the midlands and north. The southern branch seized Tara and by implication the right to nominate a king of all Ireland – *ard-rí*. Just as the *rí* who 'ruled' the *tuath* had specific and really limited powers so no one took much notice of Uí Néill's claims except as a challenge.

By the time of the firm establishment of Christianity one can associate dominant dynasties with particular parts of the island. West Ulster was the territory of the northern Uí Néill while east of the Bann (in present day County Antrim) lived the descendants of the North's original inhabitants, the Ulaid. The north midlands was known as Airgialla (a name implying hostage-giving) while north Leinster (the most fertile part of the country) was southern Uí Néill territory.

The land south of the Liffey to the southeast coast was ruled by the Laigin, always a troublesome lot, as later centuries were to show. Munster was Eoghanacht territory with a site at Cashel as numinous as Tara, and the Connacht kings of the families Uí Fiachrach and Uí Briúin claimed descent from Niall's brothers, Brión and Fiachra. Until the time of Mael Sechnaill (mid ninth century) no ruler, even of the Uí Néill, had made a formal effort to have himself declared king of Ireland, but the dynasty remained powerful for three centuries and throughout that time large tracts of the land of Ireland were under its control. Ironically it was Brian Boru, a member of an obscure *tuath* from what is now County Clare, who finally succeeded in becoming *Imperator Scottorum*.

The pre-Christian society was a hierarchical one with clear class distinctions, a fine sense of aesthetic design and an unusual respect for poetry, traditional lore (including genealogy) and storytelling. The poets shared with scholars, physicians, jurists, top artificers and scholars membership of the *aes dána* (men of art) whose social stratum was fixed between that of nobles and free commoners. In a territory where there was no 'state' the regulation of society, punishment for crime, system of inheritance, were largely the responsibility of the blood-group called the *fine* which involved collateral as well as direct descendants and baffled even the jurists in its complexity. Relationships between classes were on a client-basis, including the lowest class of the 'unfree' which numbered farm-labourers, unskilled wood and metal workers as well as captives and slaves. There was some scope for upward mobility: if a low-grade metal-worker's child developed sufficient skill he might be accepted as a free commoner and eventually as a member of the *aes dána*.

Isolation was not only desirable but easy in a country of great bogs, impenetrable woods and lakes. The people were largely self-sufficient, the poorer classes subsisting on oats, dairy products, wild fruits and nuts. Sheep provided cheese and milk as well as wool and mutton. Meat, pork, lamb, veal and wheaten bread were upper-class luxuries. Garlic, onions and kale were cultivated and freshwater fish supplemented the diet. For most people, life was like Hobbes's description of the life of primitive man everywhere, 'poor, nasty, brutish and short.' The shortness was not on the whole caused by internecine struggle. Chesterton's comment on the Gaels: 'All their wars are merry, And all their songs were sad,' is rhetorical simplification but the inter-*tuath* battles were highly formalised affairs, controlled by ritual, taboo and convention; there were many 'sanctuaries' and women, children and in time clerics were safeguarded by law. The visitations which kept the population so low were famine and pestilence which struck in each generation. There was not much in the way of surplus food and only the most primitive means of preserving and storing it, and the two apocalyptic horsemen worked well together.

The society which the Christian missionaries found was not unaware of religion. It had its gods and goddesses who lived in the Otherworld a kind of idealised life on earth where all appetites were satisfied. The people believed that death was the end only of the body and that a life of the spirit continued in another place. Their worship of the sun and the spirits of rivers and lakes indicated a pleasure in the natural world and this characterised their vernacular poetry when they found the means to write it down. They made their ancestors into heroes and their heroes into gods. When Patrick and the other missionaries brought Christianity, the Irish recognised a belief not at all alien. They took to it in time and subtly altered its practice to suit their temperaments. Their attitude to life, in so far as we can judge it, was on the whole honourable, cheerful and sensual. Divorce was prevalent and the practice of polygamy among the noble class persisted until Tudor times. In general their theology was wary but not fearful. The coming of Christianity made changes but assimilation even in this continued as a characteristic. The Gaelic way of life, modified and sensitised by the adopted faith, survived the Norman invasion and persisted in three-quarters of the country until the end of the sixteenth century. We feel that influence still: as Sean O'Faolain put it in his superlative monograph *The Irish* (1947), it has given us: 'that old atavistic individualism which tends to make all Irishmen inclined to respect no laws at all; and though this may be socially deplorable it is humanly admirable, and makes life much more tolerable and charitable and easy-going and entertaining.'

2

Christian Ireland

In fact in an oblique way Rome did conquer Ireland – not the pagan Rome of the highly trained armies and the superb engineers but the Rome of Christian missionaries who brought the faith that had come with official tolerance in the declining empire. Christianity had penetrated to western Gaul and southern England and Wales, and it was from an unsteady Roman Britain that the faith came to Celtic Ireland. The prime mover in consolidation was St Germanus of Auxerre. He had successfully preached down the Pelagian heresy in Britain and it was he who, deputed by the pope, St Celestine I, felt that the western Celtic island should have the benefits of the true faith. He had some awareness of the nature of Gaelic belief and, though some of its practices were abhorrent, he nevertheless considered that the people who were guided by the priestly cast of Druids with its animistic elements would not find Christianity too shockingly alien.

The first name associated with the Christian missionary effort was Palladius, a close friend of Celestine. He was sent as the first bishop to 'those who believe in Christ', the Christians already there. The distance to Ireland from Wales and Scotland was not daunting to fifth-century or sixth-century mariners. Though the Gaels led largely self-sufficient agricultural and pastoral lives we must assume that the inhabitants who lived on the east coast used the sea for trading or raiding. With oar and sail many braved the rough crossing in both directions. St Columban (*c.* 540–615), who with his twelve companions including St Gall brought the faith back to Germany, southern Gaul, Switzerland and northern Italy, even wrote a poem (in Latin, of course) that was an early barcarolle and contains the stirring line: '*Heia viri! nostrum reboans echo sonet heia!*' ('Come on, men! Let us make the echoes sound!'). Not all were as tough or as hotheaded as he (and he paid the price in dereliction by many of his neophytes) but crossing narrow seas went with the territory. There were considerable numbers of Irish (originating from the south coast) living in west Wales, and the Dál Riata of northeast Ulster had skipped across the North Channel to good effect, establishing a colony that was to lead to a united kingdom of Scotland. In the same way Britons speaking a different kind of Celtic had established themselves in eastern Ireland. Palladius's mission seems to have been confined to Leinster and his clients probably included emigrants from Britain.

The most significant crossing was that of the followers of Niall of the Nine Hostages (in some traditions the half-mythic man himself) who on a significant raid took prisoner Patricius, the son of Calpurnius, deacon and civil servant, a Christian Romanised Briton. The barbarians who tipped the creaky Roman empire over into chaos did not all come from the east. The story of Patrick has been the source of much piety and considerably more controversy but at least he has left documents, the most reassuring thing you can offer an historian. *Confessio* and *Epistola ad Milites Corotici* establish him as a real person from whom it is possible to shake the accretion of the hagiography of later ages. The land of Ireland, at least north of a line from Galway to Wexford, became full of what are correctly called Patrician sites (an epithet, incidentally, that jolts the classicist used to its Roman significance).

The *Confession* describes Patrick's capture, his six-year captivity in either Antrim or Mayo, depending on your chauvinism, his escape and his dream in which 'a man called Victor' gave him 'many letters' from the Irish begging him: ' . . . *ut venias et adhuc ambulas inter nos*' ('come and walk among us again'). The short book really provides little information apart from the fact that Patrick was, as he said, but an unpolished Latinist, unidentifiable placenames (his home, *Bannavem Taberniae* and *Silva Vocluti*, the place of his captivity) and his steadfast belief in the faith that he brought from Gaul. The *Letter to Coroticus's Soldiers* is full of stern rebuke of those men of a so-called Christian prince who killed Irish converts.

The faith that Patrick brought was parochial and episcopal, but as it turned out monasticism suited the Irish better both socially and psychologically. It is now agreed that the Gaulish, essentially the universal, pattern of Church organisation was stronger and the Irish bishops more powerful than was previously thought but the eremetic tradition struck an answering note in the Gaelic temperament, in spite of or because of the obvious sensuality of their culture. The episcopal system depended on metropolitans, bishops who presided over a province of lesser prelates, and this implied the existence of some kind of urban centre. Such did not exist in Ireland until the Norsemen established them in Dublin, Waterford and Limerick. The only settlements before that were accretions to the monastic sites. This lack of metropolis as much as the place's legendary reputation may have been the reason for Patrick's selection of Emain Macha as the centre of his mainly northern establishment (if indeed it was he who chose it). It was at least an identifiable centre.

The slow Christianisation of Ireland and the assimilation of Brehon laws and Druidic lore seem to have been achieved without bloodshed. They were accomplished, however, in a small country where internecine conflict, though ritualised, was endemic. One reason for the growth of a monastic structure may be that the grouping of individual huts within a stockade replicated the characteristically isolated Celtic settlements. In some cases they grew large, forming what were in fact university campuses that in time attracted students from the various British kingdoms and from Gaul. Such a foundation as Clonmacnoise might have passed for a village because of its population of religious, students and those providing ancillary services. It was as if with the coming of the monks the *tuath* had found an intellectual, social and administrative centre; the monastic settlement could well contain its prison, hospital, church, and its abbot was the spiritual equivalent of the *rí*. From the tenth century onwards the enclosures would have contained the characteristic free-standing belltower which with its impregnable walls, door set high above ground level and conical top became the characteristic Irish icon. Many compounds would have cross-slabs and, later on, high crosses which acted as a kind of pictorial bible.

As we have seen the Celtic family-group, the *fine*, was closeknit but not nuclear. It gave a man a sense of familial association that bridged five generations and inculcated a sense of very local patriotism that had a significant effect on the Gaelic system and was to persist until Tudor times. (The women had membership of the *fine* by marriage or blood connection.) It also meant that separation from the unit was in effect an exile. This was the origin of the phrase 'white martyrdom' that was voluntarily undertaken by some of the more austere monks: 'when he gives up all that is dear to him for God's sake'. The stories of Irish monks standing up to their necks in ice-cold water seem less unlikely when one considers the monastic remains on Sceilg Mhíchil off the Kerry coast. But even there St Fionán was in Irish territory and on the rare days of fair weather the green homeland could be seen. A much greater martyrdom was to leave Ireland and go to Britain or Europe as a *'perigrinator pro Christo* (an exile for Christ)'.

Not a monk himself (though there is a tradition that he lived as one for a period) Patrick is credited with extreme self-mortification, spending a biblical forty days in a tiny island in Lough Derg in County Donegal and a further forty on top of Croagh Patrick wresting promises from heaven for his beloved Irish. These literally purgatorial traditions have held fast for fifteen hundred years, providing a pair of medieval pilgrimages that will surely last into the third millennium of Christian belief. The sense of the shortness of human life and the possible length of purgatorial expiation, to say nothing of the prospect of the hell of the damned, oppressed the religious of the time. These millennial preoccupations are easily understood in the spirit of apocalypse that was clearly afflicting the western Roman empire. Yet in a way they were liberating compared with older Celtic beliefs. Christianity, at least, had precise views about heaven and hell, as to how to attain one and avoid the other.

As it turned out the first Nordic invasion of the Angles, Saxons and Jutes, like the Romans, stopped at the Irish Sea. The amenities of the civilisation that these tribes obliterated helped with the destruction; the Roman roads simply made the conquest easier. Yet the faith that was the gift of the western empire was secure in the western island and it was Irishmen like Colum Cille of Iona and Aidan of Lindisfarne who brought it back to a not unwilling people in Scotland and Northumbria. The faith they preached was in essence that of Pope St Gregory I and his missionary to the 'non *Angli, sed angeli*', Augustine of Canterbury, but certain Irish monastic practices to do with tonsures and the computation of the date of Easter were to cause a rift that shook a few ecclesiastical belfries and had formally and finally to be settled at the Synod of Whitby in 664. The monks of Irish establishments in England accepted the synodal judgement but some of the insular fathers, notably those in Iona (with the exception of Adomnan the abbot), and Colmán, persisted in maintaining the old ways. The last resistance to the Roman practice had died out by the end of the eighth century and by then there were more serious considerations for the Church as a second barbarian invasion began to shake the Christian isles.

Monasticism had begun in the Church with the 'desert fathers' who took Christ's counsels of perfection literally. A typical eremite was St Antony (251–356) who lived in the Egyptian desert and spent his time in prayer, study and necessary manual work. In time he was joined by disciples, upon whom he imposed a simple rule. The idea of a community came from such small beginnings, although Antony at the age of about sixty left to live alone again in a cave in northern Egypt for his remaining forty years of apparently healthy life. The coenobitic (literally 'community living') movement spread east and west and came to Ireland partly from Wales, in the persons of Finnian of Clonard, Aidan of Ferns, Senan of Scattery Island (near Kilrush, County Clare) and Brendan of Clonfert, who had been trained by Illtyd of Caldey and Wales's patron, David of Mynyw, and partly from Scotland from the famous *Candida Casa* of St Ninian on the coast of Galloway, near modern Stranraer. The northern founders included Enda of Aran, who is credited with the establishment of the first Irish monastery and the imposition of the extreme ascetic rule, Tighernagh of Clones, Coirpre of Coleraine and most significant, Finnian of Movilla, who was Colum Cille's tutor.

It was customary for each monk to have his own cell, though there were exceptions, with the abbot, who was most likely in holy orders, occupying one slightly larger and set at a distance from the others. The cells were made of wood or the staple Celtic material of wattle and daub and have long disappeared. The Irish 'desert fathers', however, took to western coasts and islands where there were no trees and made their 'beehive' cells of stone, which may still be seen, notably in Sceilg Mhíchíl. In the 'golden age' of peaceful monasticism the monastery palisade would have enclosed among other buildings a scriptorium where the scriptures were copied and the illuminated manuscripts that were the glory of Christian Ireland's first millennium were created. The monks wore tunics covered by a hooded woollen robe called a *casula* and their controversial tonsure consisted of shaving the front of the scalp up to the crown of the head. Manual labour was an important part of the day, which was long and broken by no more than two meals, largely vegetarian. Lent, Advent and the forty days after Pentecost were times of great austerity, while Wednesdays and Fridays were days of special mortification.

One notable characteristic of Irish monasticism was that the monks did not belong to a particular order: there was no mother house, no abbot-general. Variations in rule were common, depending upon the decision of the local abbot. The rule devised by Columban was exemplarily severe and sprang most likely from the austerity he had experienced during his novitiate in Bangor under Comgall. His insistence upon it and on Irish practices brought him into controversy with Pope Gregory, more than fifty years before Whitby.

Though the main study of the monks was the sacred books and commentaries, profane literature began to flourish as well. The Celts, like the Norsemen who tried to destroy their civilisation, were illiterate. Apart from a primitive alphabetical system of grooves on the edges of stones called *ogham* which sufficed for sepulchral memorials, they had no means of rendering their vast store of knowledge. The lore of the *aes dána*, the cultured class, had been preserved in prodigious feats of memorising and the habit persisted long after the coming of writing. The absurdly complicated Brehon laws and the hero stories of the Gaels had replaced written history. Memory is not precise and is as creative as other aspects of the imagination. The coming of Latin uncial provided a means of recording this vernacular culture and the great hero cycles, which told of such demigods as Medb, Cu Chulainn, Deirdre, Fionn and the Red Branch Knights, were finally written down and formalised. The island's half-remembered, half-imagined early history, its laws, traditions, religious beliefs were recorded in a series of Great Books which have preserved what was understood about Ireland and its past by contemporaries from the coming of Christianity up to the time of the Tudor destruction of the Gaelic civilisation. A tradition of poetry flourished, appearing first as idle doodles on the margin of religious manuscripts. Its main themes were God and nature, flora and fauna, the year's turning – all characteristic of a people which lived as much as possible out of doors – but ribaldry and wit and delight in the grotesque played their parts too.

The old monks also helped to preserve a delight in the works of classical antiquity and they played their parts in the re-education of a Europe that had grown dark with barbarian intrusion. Colum Cille and Columban were only the first and most famous of a series of religious who brought not only sacred knowledge but liberal learning. Alcuin, who was trained by Irish monks in Northumbria, became Charlemagne's minister of education and one of the greatest preservers and advancers of the humanities in the middle ages. Sedulius Scottus (*c.* 820–c.880) and Johannes Scotus Eriugena (*c.* 810–c.870) both labelled Irish, the latter twice over, lead the list of *docti* who were the glory of pre-Renaissance Europe and who gave their homeland the justifiable title of a land of scholars.

The period from the acceptance of Christianity until the first coming of the Vikings is usually regarded as a golden age, though the country was still as vulnerable to the twin visitations of famine and pestilence as it had been in the fifth century. Struggles between rival dynasties continued, often with clerics in the opposing armies. There is a strong tradition that even so saintly a man as Colum Cille was sufficiently susceptible to his position as a noble member of the Cenél Conaill to have taken part in the battle of Cúl Dreimhne as a prelude to his leaving Ireland to found the great monastery of Iona. The battle was fought against the Connachta *c.* 562, appropriately enough under Ben Bulben, a groyne that geographically and mythically separates Connacht from Ulster.

Still the monasteries continued to flourish, combining

23

aesthetics with worship. It was the period of the great *Book of Kells* (made in Iona and brought home to Mide to save it from the Norse marauders), the Ardagh chalice, the Athlone crucifixion plaque, the high crosses and the other glories of Irish art. It was also a period of the preservation and growth of learning recorded in beautiful written and sumptuously produced books. By the time the first Scandinavian pirates appeared off Lindisfarne, Iona and Rathlin in the last decade of the eighth century, there had been a tradition of love of learning, appreciation of beauty and delight in the chronicling of romance and high deeds for nearly a millennium. The natural inclinations of the people had been enhanced by the Christian missionaries and Ireland shone like a beacon of faith and learning in an umbrous Europe.

3

Vikings and High Kings

Whether the early immigrants whose arrivals were told as wonder tales by the Gaelic chroniclers came as colonists, conquerors or opportunists is not clear, but the marauders who broke the long peace in the last decade of the eighth century certainly came for plunder. (The term 'peace' is probably a misnomer because internal struggles continued with only slight mitigation brought by the influence of the Church.) The Scandinavians were the great amphibious people of Europe and they were cruel and efficient warriors. The Swedes looked eastward and, penetrating into the heart of Russo/Slav territory, founded the cities of Novgorod and Kiev; the Danes concentrated on the North Sea and, conquering most of eastern and midland England, founded in their Danelaw a dynasty which lasted until 1042. It was perhaps ironic that William the Conqueror, who broke the power of the residual Danes and Anglo-Saxons in 1066, was himself the ruler of a people descended from Norse invaders who arrived three hundred years before Hastings. This atavistic relationship no doubt made it easy for Duke

William to persuade Harald Hardrada, King of Norway, to invade northern England and force Harold the Saxon to meet and defeat him at Stamford Bridge a mere three weeks before he had to face William's invaders.

The Norwegian warriors were the fiercest, the most adventurous and the ones who, taking the 'outer line', did most initial harm to Ireland. There were some Danes in southern Ireland (occasionally routes crossed) but it was mainly Norsemen who sacked the monasteries (the only settlements that these instinctive town-builders could see) that contained the gold and bejewelled chalices, monstrances and lay ornaments that were the country's pride and the source of its international reputation. They also had bodies who could be taken as slaves or hostages for ransom. The Gaelic Church's predilection for building their holy structures on islands or sea-capes made the pirates' task easier. Lindisfarne was attacked in 793, Rathlin, Lambay and Iona assailed in 795 and Iona fired in 802 and attacked again in 806 when more than sixty of the monks were killed.

The causes of the Scandinavian excursus were complex. Overpopulation was a significant one; in Norway especially there was little arable land and though there may have been *Lebensraum* enough there was a distinct lack of *Lebensmittel*. Important too was the odd raiding-and-trading mixture in the Nordic psyche. There was a warrior tradition, sedulously reinforced by womenfolk who often accompanied their men on raids, but there was an equally deep instinct to use their nautical skills for trade and this implied the establishment of depots which inevitably grew into towns. Perhaps the most significant element was that the time was ripe. The sea-raiders had developed magnificent warships, elegant in their long curving lines and clinker-built to withstand the buffeting of Atlantic waves and the rip tides between the western islands. These with their bright colours, sealed with the copper-based paint from midland Sweden, their dragon-headed prows and their bows armoured with hanging shields were enough to terrify armies, let alone undefended monks. The ferocity of the invaders, which included rape and the mutilation of the ribs and lungs of live captives into the 'blood eagle' was proverbial, and had the effect, in Ireland at least, of increasing the bloodiness of response and the conduct of internal wars.

The nature of the Irish mainland could not have been better designed for Viking inroads. The ships were of sufficiently shallow draught for them to sail up the Shannon beyond Clonmacnoise, to row up the lower Bann and anchor in Lough Neagh. The Slaney, Barrow, Nore, Suir, Blackwater all were navigable and Lough Foyle, Belfast Lough, the bays of Dublin and Galway and the harbours of Wexford, Waterford and Cork made landings and settlement comparatively easy. The taking of Iceland, Shetland, Orkney, the Inner and Outer Hebrides, Ross, Galloway and Dumfries, and the establishment of Ostman (as the *Lochlannaigh* called themselves) Irish east coast settlements, made the northern approaches to the western isles Scandinavian and the Irish Sea a Norse lake with the Isle of Man as a convenient tactical and mercantile centre.

The eighth- and early ninth-century moves were mainly

booty raids, as were those to the east, west and south of Europe. In 837, however, a large fleet appeared at the Boyne and Dublin Bay, and the Vikings, united under a ruthless leader Thorgestr, laid waste most of the midland foundations, having set up a permanent camp at the ford near the mouth of the Liffey. In 841 Thorgestr took his fleet up the Bann and anchored in Lough Neagh, whence it was comparatively easy to lay waste the north. In 844 he established his fleet and his marines in Lough Ree, which gave him a base for the devastation of Mide and Connachta. His race was finally stopped when Máel-Shechlainn I captured him and drowned him in Lough Owel. (This was the Malachy of Tom Moore's melody, 'Let Erin Remember' who 'wore the collar of gold/ Which he won from the proud invader'.)

The Irish were slow to respond to the proud invaders. The nature of the island's political structure made it very difficult to organise a united front against them. Though the earlier raiders had relied on sword, arrow and spear and wore no armour, later waves came equipped with helmets and chain-mail. Their ships when in battle array were, in a sense, 'ironclad' and the marines were trained to fight in an adamantine wedge formation which made it hard for the forces of the local king to break and scatter. The Irish had not much sea power, though they defeated a Viking force in a sea battle in Lough Foyle in 833. Derry was probably not rich enough to attract the marauders but they appeared in Lough Foyle, as the placename Dún na Long indicates; it was probably the site of a *longphort* (shipstead) made by drawing up the longships on to the shore and making of them a fortified encampment. The effective response of the Cenél Eogháin kings of Aileach at different times during the ninth and tenth centuries helped to show that the Lochlannaigh, could be stopped but this was probably not to the ultimate advantage of Derry. If the Vikings had been allowed to establish a town on the Foyle, as they did on the Liffey, Suir, Slaney, Lee and Shannon, the isolation of Gaelic Ulster might not have been as complete.

Máel-Shechlainn's success with Thorgestr enabled him to claim Tara and the name of *ard-rí*, and only part of his energies were directed against the 'Gall' (the opposite of 'Gael' – a name for foreigner that was to be applied thereafter to Ireland's colonisers). During his reign (846-62) the Ostmen had caught the Irish fever sufficiently to engage in alliances with native kings. Aed Finnleith, king of the northern Uí Néill, who successfully cleared the Vikings from the north coast in 866, had earlier made an alliance with Dublin Danes. In the summers of 914 and 915 huge fleets arrived at Waterford and Wexford. It was clear that a second and more powerful drive was going to be made on the land of Leinster and Munster. The attacks on monasteries at Cork and Lismore were as savage as any in the previous century. Again the marauders met with little or no resistance until another overking of the Uí Néill, Niall Glúndub, collected a host from Ulster, Meath and Connacht, and met the Viking forces under Ragnall and Sitric. In 919 he and many of his finest warriors were killed at the battle of Islandbridge, upriver from Dublin. The next score years saw the rooting-in of Ostman settlements and the creation of towns out of what had merely been winter encampments. The Liffey settlement would have become even stronger had not the Dublin Vikings (a mixture of Dane and Norse) been preoccupied with their larger settlement at Yorvick, the modern York, which needed protection from Northumbria in the north and from Mercia in the west. The other settlements, especially those in Waterford and Limerick, prospered.

Indeed by mid-century, the Limerick Ostmen had become Christian and their king Ímar had begun to engage in the dangerous business of Irish politics. As ever combining raiding with trading, he made frequent forays into the surrounding countryside. The story of these events of the second half of the tenth century are told in *Cogad Gaedel re Gallaib* (*War of the Irish with the Foreigners*) which describes the career of Brian Boru ('Brian of the tributes'). (The document was commissioned by the twelfth-century O'Briens who regarded this Irish hero as their ancestor.) He was the son of Cennetig, the leader of the tiny *tuath* Dál Cais in east Clare, who died in 951 to be succeeded by his elder son Mathgamain. Their main adversaries were not the Ostmen but the Eoghanacht, who were traditional rulers of Munster with their spiritual and social centre at Cashel. Mathgamain captured the rocky citadel in 964 and two years later with the help of his younger brother's specially trained Dalcassian army defeated at Sulchoid the Norse of Limerick, who were Eoghanacht allies, and sacked their city. Mathgamain was killed, not in open battle or by challenge and therefore 'treacherously', by Ímar's soldiers in 976, and his brother exacted a swift revenge which involved the sacrilegious disregard of sanctuary when he killed Ímar and his sons in the church of Scattery Island.

Within three years Brian ruled Limerick and Munster. In 997, he outfaced Máel Sechnaill, the king of the southern Uí Néill, who had till then ambitions to become *ard rí* in fact as well as name, and they made a formal division of the land of Ireland between them. At the battle of Tara in 980, Máel Sechnaill vanquished the Norse of Dublin and the following year he sacked the city. The Leinstermen and their Ostman allies fell to the Clare champion at Glen Máma in 999, but an expected confrontation between the high king and Brian did not take place, and by 1002 Ireland had an overall ruler.

For at least ten years Brian reigned almost undisputed as king of Ireland, though it was necessary from time to time to cow some dissident northern kings. The time has been glamorised by romantic nineteenth-century writers as a kind of Camelot with the Irish Arthur making good the Viking depredations, restoring the Church to its elevated position in society and advancing art and learning. All legends are true in some ways and myths are just generalised biography. No modern historian would agree to Brian's canonisation, even though the icon of his death at the hands of Brodir illustrated school textbooks and adorned many parochial halls. This picture of the crowned king falling to 'Dane' swords had as its focus the crucifix upon the camp table; it was, after all, Good Friday. Hagiography aside, Brian seems to have been a practising Christian and understood the need for a spiritual element in the stable society he was attempting to build. His confirmation of the primacy of Armagh was not just a matter of policy, though it was an appropriate place to have himself inscribed as *Imperator Scottorum*. His tour of the north the following year, establishing that title and taking the hostages which gave him his tributary sobriquet, was essentially a triumphal progress and a necessary step in the ambitious process which might have made Ireland a united and cohesive country before any of its insular neighbours.

Though historians now tend to undervalue the part played by individuals in what they see as the true causes of events, we should perhaps scandalously mention the woman Gormflath (Kormlada in the Norse saga) whose career, like that of Nesta of Wales and Dervorgilla of Meath, gives colour to otherwise dull accounts of dynastic struggles. She was mother of Sigtrygger aka Sitric (who ruled Dublin until 1036 and married Brian's daughter) but married in turn Máel Sechnaill and the aging Brian himself and bore the latter a son. Both these Irish husbands in time repudiated her and it is likely that the main spur of her career was dynastic power and the advancement of the kingdom of Leinster, that power enjoyed vicariously through her son and her brother Máel Mórda, who between them ruled all the land of the southeastern province. It is too simplistic to suggest that it was her taunts of vassalage that stirred up her brother and son against the great king but no doubt they gave further weight to their reasons for defiance.

The imperial peace was shattered in 1012 by the Ostmen-

Leinster alliance made bold by promises of help from Viking cousins in Man, the Hebrides, Orkneys and Iceland. (The contemporary equivalent of the tabloid press insisted that the beautiful baleful Gormflath offered herself as an extra enticement to Sigurd, the leader of the allies, much as Medb did to Dáire mac Fiachna as part-payment for the Brown Bull of Cuailgne.) Brian and his son Murchad fought a war of attrition until, in the spring of 1014, Máel Mórda and Sitric and their allies met the forces of Brian on the high ground near the Tolka with Máel Sechnaill's army kept behind the battle lines as a second wave. This proved unnecessary. Brian was in his early seventies but still a superb tactician. Murchad smashed the allies' line and Sigurd and Máel Mórda were killed. It was a gang of fleeing Norse who stumbled upon the unprotected king in his campaign tent. The battle was fierce and formed a significant section of the Viking saga of *Burnt Njal*. Brian's heir and most efficient captain Murchad and his son Turloch died, and only Sitric, who had watched the battle from the walls of the pocket city, survived to rule as king of Dublin.

Clontarf was not the battle that broke Viking power in Ireland; that was already in decline, or rather it was sloughing off its bellicosity and in the process of being assimilated into the only minimally xenophobic country. Brian won the battle but with his death and that of his effective heir the prospect of a united Ireland died too. Máel Sechnaill, who had left the field of Clontarf, reigned as high king until his death in 1022. Brian's remaining sons were weak and indecisive and the might of the Dalcassians shrank and their territory eventually became that of the O'Briens of Thomond. The reign of Brian was a fleeting wisp of glory and the nature of the Irish state was again that of inter-*tuath* wars, now more efficiently and bloodily prosecuted, and often so protracted that the beginnings of a rudimentary civil service was observable. With kings of the warring regions, now about one hundred and fifty in number, in the field or in siege for months at a time, the domestic affairs of *tuatha* were overseen by royal stewards and bailiffs and the ideal of a high king of Ireland who would rule a united and peaceful country was as chimerical as ever. Yet there was the makings of another Brian in Toirdelbach Ua Conchobair (Turloch O'Conor) who, coming out of Connacht, imposed his will sufficiently on his rivals to become high king. He fought and ruled for fifty years from 1106 until in 1156 his son Ruaidrí (Rory) acceded to the kingship. The Ua Conchobair dynasty looked as if it might realise Brian's earlier ambition of a compact kingdom. Ruaidrí, like Brian's Donnchad, was not of the quality of his father. He was to be the last high king of Ireland and no match for the Leinster king Diarmait Mac Murchada (Dermot MacMurrough) and his Gall allies.

Historical speculation is vain, a kind of otiose parlour game, but it is interesting to consider what difference a strong and cohesive Ireland might have made in the history of the second half of the eleventh century. The conquest of Anglo-Saxon England might have occurred through the Severn estuary and Gaelic rather than Norman French become the language of the Irish court at Bristol. Certainly, strong island kingdoms instinctually feel the need for expansion. However, the shock of the Viking depredations took a long time to disperse. Many abuses, including the ecclesiastical, already rife in the ninth-century and allowed to persist and worsen during the more than two centuries of social disruption, were blamed on the Scandinavian terror. The unknown monk whose oft-quoted doodle in praise of stormy nights records his awareness of savage warriors crossing the Irish Sea might also have been at risk from his own kind. Feidlimid mac Crimhthain, king-bishop of Cashel, is reputed to have destroyed more Church property than any foreigner.

The hundred and fifty years between 'Brian's battle' and the appearance of the Cambro-Normans at Bannow was marked by Church reform as well as dynastic struggle. Ireland was still a land of scholars and artificers, of poets and masons. By the time Leinster, ever the contrary region, was ready to wreck the frail unity the country had attained, a reformed Church was again a patron of the arts and an intellectual conduit from Europe. The Ostmen had brought towns and the expertise to make them prosperous and, as Gaelic-speaking and Christian, acceptable to all. Learning, as ever, flourished, and more elaborate churches and monasteries rose. The literati of the time had their own epic romance in the twelfth-century literary text *Acallam na senórach* (*The Colloquy of the Elders*), by coincidence published about the same time as Geoffrey of Monmouth's *History of the Kings of Britain* which started the Arthurian craze. The stories of the Fianna and the star-crossed lovers, Diarmuit and Gráinne, with the glory of ancient days, chivalric heroes and the joys of noble combat and hunting subtly adapted to suit the growing sophistication of the time, were in notable contrast to the murkiness of the political life of the period, but as in Renaissance Italy civil unrest did not obliterate aesthetics and many parts of Ireland had periods of peace. But the distressful country was now to face another invasion of the Gall, this time with consequences that affect the country still.

4

The Creek of Baginbun

When one considers the British Isles, it appears that there is a certain inevitability about their history. By the time the inhabitants of England, Scotland, Wales and Ireland had a firm perception of their identity and separateness, confrontation and struggle were inevitable. Their being cut off from the mainland of Europe aggravated the condition. Once the Normans had secured the vassalage of the Anglo-Saxons and established a sort of peace in England, it was clear that it was much the richest and strongest of the four countries, especially since it had half of France behind it. Relations with Scotland and Wales were a significant element of Norman statecraft and, rather as they were to do a century later in Ireland, the Franks quickly annexed as much of southern Wales and Scotland as they could take without too much opposition. As early as 1070 William I had delivered over the border territories to 'marcher' lords, who gradually extended their domains to the point where they constituted a threat to the central government. The north of Wales remained Celtic and there were regular insurrections until Edward I completed the conquest in 1283. He had less success with the Scots, who after a series of revolts led by Wallace and Bruce finally defeated the English at Bannock-burn in 1314. Relations between the two kingdoms continued turbulent for the next three centuries, until the accession of James VI (I of England) in 1603.

The detached island had come under Norman scrutiny in the reigns of William I and his son Henry I, but no moves were made. William's great-grandson Henry II was the first English king to involve himself in Irish affairs and at the time he came more out of necessity than for colonisation. He had taken out in 1155 the most potent *laissez-passer* of the time, a letter from the pope. This was the bull *Laudabiliter* which granted the island of Ireland to Henry as if he were a kind of latter-day Patrick. Duke William had obtained a similar licence from Alexander II to go and civilise the Anglo-Saxons and Danes. It was, after all, the age of crusades, and the Irish were savage and ungovernable. Even the saintly Malachy had complained about their vices and lack of conformity to universal Church practice. That Adrian IV, who granted the bull, was an Englishman, Nicholas Breakspear, is mere coincidence, but this awkward fact gave rise to much recrimination and bitterly voiced doubts about its authenticity in the eight centuries since.

Yet for Henry II it was not much more than a indication of intent. His reign was turbulent and relations with later popes far from cordial. Ireland was not his chiefest pre-occupation until he realised that his venturesome barons were beginning to become too powerful after the success of their Irish caper. The beginning of the Irish adventure was accidental, passionate and even operatic in its stimulus, and not untypical of its source. The bull had given Henry permission to subject the Irish people to law, to root out from them 'the weeds of vice' and 'proclaim the truths of the Church to a rude and ignorant people'. The language is full of paternalistic unction and no more accurate about the Irish people than that of any later improver of the heathen with Bible and gun.

There had been abuses in the Church but St Malachy (Máel Maedoc), when archbishop of Armagh, had set in motion the means of reformation long before his death in 1148. The European style of monasticism, which he introduced with the setting up of a Cistercian abbey at Mellifont, went a long way to remove the abuses of secularism and married clergy that had bedevilled the older foundations, when many abbeys were family affairs. Dioceses were disentangled from abbey domains and bishops generally replaced abbots as the ecclesiastical rulers of the *tuath* clusters which had been ruled in pre-Christian times by a *ruire* (over-king). The regulations about marriage and divorce, once based on the Brehon Laws, were brought in line with the Hildebrandian reforms elsewhere and the Irish Church was more 'European' and therefore Roman than she had been for hundreds of years. Malachy's horror tales of Irish vileness to St Bernard of Clairvaux, his soul-friend, were emotional outbursts and not affidavits but to the ears of Eugenius III and his successor Adrian they were reason enough to authorise conquest.

The charge of rudeness and ignorance was not true at all;

as ever strangeness was interpreted as barbarism. The culture of Ireland was not so much European as, perhaps, Mediterranean. The twelfth-century Irish versions of stories of antiquity are the oldest in non-classical languages. It was in this era that the oral versions of the great pagan sagas, such as *Táin bó Cuailgne,* were written down by clerical scribes. The tradition of native poetry was well established and it was social as well as religious, epigrammatic as well as celebratory. The reforms of Malachy and his ilk pleased Rome and the episcopal hierarchies but their imposition was not effected without damage to the magnificent institutions which were the source of Irish culture, the island's intellectual powerhouses. The ironic effect of the dissolution of the old Irish monasteries was laicisation of academic and aesthetic life. The secular trend was accelerated by the disruption which followed the Norman invasion, but Ireland's golden age of unabashed scholarship had succumbed to saintliness.

Outside the cloisters the country was still a ragbag of warring kingdoms. The prospect of a once and future king was as elusive as ever. Ruaidrí O'Connor had become *ard rí* on the death of the great Turloch, but his position was heavily dependent upon the support of others who were near-rivals. One of these was the one-eyed king of Bréifne, Tighearnán O'Rourke (Ruairc) whose wife the Meath princess Dervorgilla (Dearbhfhorgaill) was to become the catalyst for catastrophe. The problem, as ever, originated in Leinster and was partially rooted in the otherness of Dublin. Its clergy owed allegiance to Canterbury and not to Armagh, even after the reformed diocesan structures were in place;

it did not become fully incorporated into the Irish hierarchy until 1152. Its first Irish archbishop, St Laurence O'Toole (Lorcán Ua Tuathail), was taken unwillingly from his abbacy of Glendalough in 1161 and indeed he was to play a significant part in the politics of the city and the adjacent kingdom. As a child he had been held as a hostage at the court of Dermot MacMurrough, who later became his brother-in-law, though he can hardly have approved of many of MacMurrough's activities.

Dublin's trade with Bristol and ports of France had acquainted it with the Anglo-Norman world and it tended to look east rather than west. The gradual consciousness among the Irish kings of its evident destiny made it a prize worth the fighting for. It was already regarded by MacMurrough as his own property and this typical piece of presumption made it necessary that Ruaidrí O'Connor, who became *ard rí* (in fact the last to bear that title) in 1166, should prevent the presumption from becoming actuality. The animus against MacMurrough was intensified by the Dervorgilla adventure. In 1151 MacMurrough had carried her off, probably by invitation – they were the media stars of the time – thus earning the undying hatred of her husband, the lord of Bréifne. This enmity was not at all mitigated by his sending her home again. (She died in 1193 in the Cistercian Abbey of Mellifont that she had lavishly endowed.)

The combined forces of O'Rourke and O'Connor, supplemented by an army from Dublin and the Norsemen from Wexford, dethroned MacMurrough and destroyed his castle at Ferns. He sailed for Bristol on 1 August 1166, taking with him a few followers and his daughter Aoife, whose position and beauty made her a substantial matrimonial prize. When MacMurrough finally met Henry II (in southern France) the king accepted his fealty and gave him permission to canvass what aid he could from his subjects. Ireland still did not concern him; his struggle with Thomas à Becket had begun and his empire stretching 'from the Cheviots to the Pyrenees' required that he spend as much time in France as in England. MacMurrough found support among the Welsh-Norman lords, two at least of whom, Maurice Fitzgerald and Robert Fitzstephen, were the children of Nesta ap Rhys, the fertile and bounteous princess of Wales. Their leader was Richard de Clare, Earl of Pembroke, more commonly known as 'Strongbow', whom MacMurrough invited to become his son-in-law with right of succession to his Leinster territories.

The force that landed on 1 May 1169 at Bannow Bay in southern Wexford comprised 'Robert Fitzstephen, Maurice Prendergast, thirty knights, sixty men at arms and three hundred archers'. They were joined by Dermot, quickly secured Wexford and soon established a reputation for efficiency and cruelty. Dermot had been in Ireland since 1167 and he had already made a temporary accommodation with O'Connor and O'Rourke. He could afford to wait, for his adversaries did not seem to understand the threat to the whole country that the foreigners constituted. The soldiers of Strongbow were probably the most effective fighting force in the Europe of the time. They were mainly Welsh and Flemings, who had a fearsome reputation as archers, and the cavalry was the best in the Angevin Empire. Most wore mail suits and the mounted knights had long shields, conical helmets with protective nose-pieces and long lances. The lightly-clad Irish who fought on the ground with axes, swords and slings were no match for them. The Normans maintained their conquests by building fortresses, though the early ones were simply man-made mounds topped by wooden towers and surrounded by protective ditches and walls of wood and stone – the 'motte and bailey'. The stone castles, ruins of which are still such a feature of the south and east, came later.

In May 1170, in response to Dermot's urgent messages, Strongbow, not yet ready to sail, sent as an advance guard another of his lieutenants, Raymond le Gros. He landed at the rocky head of Baginbun at the southwest point of Bannow. His small force first threw up defensive earth works and defeated a combined force of Waterford Norse and Irish from the Decies numbering a supposed 3,000 (the figures are from Norman chronicles). As the old rhyme put it:

> At the creek of Baginbun
> Was Ireland lost and Ireland won.

The shock troops took Waterford and reinforced their reputation for extreme cruelty by breaking the limbs of seventy leading citizens of the town and throwing them into the sea. Strongbow himself landed on 23 August and the promised marriage to Aoife was solemnised in the cathedral. By the time of MacMurrough's sudden death in 1171, he had had his lands in Leinster restored and was confirmed as lord of Dublin. His death was followed by a rising of Leinstermen against Strongbow which he put down quickly. Strongbow then assumed power in Dublin, henceforth the centre of foreign power in the country. After a prolonged siege of the city by the combined armies of O'Connor, O'Rourke and O'Carroll (from what is now Monaghan-Louth) who, lacking engines, could rely only on blockade, Strongbow, le Gros and Milo de Cogan in a sudden outbreak defeated their unprepared forces at Castleknock.

Strongbow was now in a position to declare himself an independent king of Leinster and Dublin with support from his lieutenants who held Wexford and Waterford. It is likely that it was the Irish themselves who first drew Henry II's attention to the power that his late minions now wielded, although he had his own sources of intelligence. He decided that the Irish adventure was not quite what he had anticipated and that he should speedily impose his authority not necessarily on Ireland but upon his unruly barons. His late friend, counsellor and ecclesiastical conscience, Thomas à Becket, the head of the English Church, had died at the hands of knights much like Strongbow's men and it was believed at the time that the murder had Henry's assent. It was an appropriate time to be out of England.

He landed with a army of 4,000 men near Waterford on 17 October 1171 and was immediately greeted by formal homage from all the Cambro-Norman freelances who had found the Irish adventure so exciting and profitable. Strongbow was granted the kingdom of Leinster to hold in fief for the king, the others received similar grants, and

Henry himself took as his personal property the kingdom of Dublin and all the Irish seaports. The great majority of Irish kings came to make formal protests of fealty, regarding him as an *ard rí* who, being an absentee, would bother them even less than the native kind. Henry also won over the Irish churchmen by calling a synod, held significantly at Cashel, at the end of the year. The main reconciliation role was played by St Laurence O'Toole, and, by the time Henry was ready to leave, the long-attempted reforms were well in place. The country had its system of parishes in dioceses, the foundations of a great cathedral had been laid in Dublin and the forms were those of Canterbury. All the lords, temporal and spiritual, had accepted the foreign king, except those of Cenél Eógain and the Cenél Conaill, who in the remote north-west were, as ever, embroiled in their own quarrels.

Henry had come to rap knuckles but he soon realised that he had in Ireland, certainly in the fertile east and the commercial cities, a worthy acquisition. The English had come to stay. Their power varied through the centuries, reaching a zenith by the end of the thirteenth century when they controlled most of the country, even parts of Ulster, but by the time of the Wars of the Roses it was confined to the land of the Pale, which comprised essentially the modern counties of Dublin, Meath and parts of Louth and Kildare. The influence of the English kings was even more fitful. Some, like John, left a firm mark upon the country. They set in motion a process which would lead to a central administration with coinage, juries, and even a parliament in 1297 (in the reign of Edward I), all steps in a lengthy progress to a unified and democratic country. Henry III, John's successor, required more and more land to be held by his Irish barons; in response, his justiciar, Maurice Fitzgerald, had taken over Connacht by 1243 and had turned his attentions to Ulster. More than a hundred years later Edward III sent his son Lionel, Duke of Clarence, to counteract the rise of the Gaelic chieftains, but the only significant achievement of his five-year stay (1361-6) was the passing of the unenforceable Statutes of Kilkenny.

The most visible presence of any king in the medieval period was that of Richard II, who landed in 1394 with the largest army ever seen up till that time. He drove Art MacMurrough out of Leinster and accepted the submission of nearly all the chiefs, both Irish and English. He returned again in 1399 to avenge the death of his heir, Roger Mortimer, who had been killed in battle – a trip which cost him his throne and eventually his life. While Richard was trying to deal with Art MacMurrough, who was by then a much better tactician, his arch-enemy, Henry of Hereford, as son of John of Gaunt a claimant to the English throne, had landed with a small army in Yorkshire and was well on the way to becoming Henry IV.

The Norman conquest of Ireland had only been partial; between the coming of Strongbow and the even less desirable attentions of Henry VIII in the mid-sixteenth century, the English kings did not pay to Ireland the attention it deserved and needed if it was to become, as England was, a homogeneous and prosperous country. Ireland remained as obstinately divided as ever, although paradoxically its mixed culture continued to flourish. The Normans brought order, amenity and a kind of civilisation, and their lands showed a graciousness and an urbanity that the rougher Gaelic tracts could not aspire to. Under them there was a peace which was in notable contrast to the Gaelic dominions, where raids and counter-offensives even between members of the same clan were the norm. The romantic historians of the last century cursed the coming of the Gall and their bringing of seven hundred years of slavery; the more realistic modern comment-ators rather argue that the British came at that time but would have come anyway. But what was lost, as so often, it seemed, at different cruxes during those centuries, was an opportunity to heal Ireland's persistent instinct for fragmentation.

5

HIBERNICIS IPSIS HIBERNIORES

The first English viceroy – the contemporary word was 'justiciar' – Hugo de Lacy was given a grant of Meath to balance the holding of Leinster by Strongbow (who lived only another five years). It was a stark indication that Henry's word was no more to be trusted than that of any other conqueror. The territory included a large tract of the midlands which was managed by de Lacy's knights, but the labour was provided by the Gaelic Irish peasants, the class as always least affected by change of leadership. The Norman Plunketts, Nugents, Daltons feudalised the territory and emphasised their control by their manors and castles. De Lacy built Trim and Drogheda, establishing a pattern that other magnates would follow in creating market towns for the effective commercial disposal of the produce of their estates. These lands were not without benefit of clergy. The new overlords were noted for their public piety and the 'lands of peace' had an abundance of clergy, secular and coenobitic. These were all faithful to Pope Alexander III who, accepting Henry's penitence for the murder of Thomas à Becket, had underwritten the terms of his predecessor's bull, *Laudabiliter*.

Munster, which soon became a kind of French province, was parcelled out among Henry's close associates: the south (Desmond) to Fitzstephen and de Cogan, Thomond to de Braose. The territory of Ulidia (the modern south Antrim and Down) was taken over by another adventurer, John de Courcy, who in 1177 (two years after the Treaty of Windsor which had guaranteed all Irish holdings), with an army of bored Dublin Normans and some Irish troops, captured Rathkeltar and renamed it Downpatrick, building a cathedral in thanksgiving. The towns of Dromore, Newry, Carlingford, Carrickfergus and Coleraine also owed their prosperous existence to de Courcy and his successors. The adventure had at least the retroactive approval of the king, but in that year he won from Alexander III the consent to appoint his troublesome youngest son John 'Lord of Ireland'. He had tried to have him made king but not even that agreeable pope would grant his request.

John found it judicious to make two visits to Ireland. The first, in 1185, was undertaken for the purpose of viewing his Irish domains and it was characterised by his offending practically everybody. He brought with him Theodore Walter, his butler, Walter de Burgo and Thomas Fitzgerald, and granted them the territories that enabled them in time to found the great Anglo-Irish families, Butler, Burke and Fitzgerald. John, now king, returned in 1210 with the intention of weakening the power of the barons (it was five years before Magna Carta) and greatly increased the power of the throne, to be mediated through a justiciar with greater authority and a greatly enlarged civil service. St Patrick's Cathedral was established partly as a kind of college to supply learned clerks for this purpose. Its academic reputation later made it the appropriate site for the medieval University of Dublin, which was founded in 1320 and lasted until 1494.

Ruaidrí O'Connor had concluded the Windsor treaty with Henry in good faith but soon found that his high kingship had shrunk to his father's old lands in Connacht. Yet even this was to fall to the unstoppable power of Norman arms. A new generation of barons, de Burgos, de Lacys, Fitzgeralds, led an army across the Shannon in 1235 and pushed as far as Westport. The towns Galway, Athenry, Dunmore, Ballinrobe and Loughrea were founded, but they always had a watchful air about them, sealed fortresses in an area where the Norman population was sparse. By 1250, four-fifths of the country had been taken by the Gall. Even Inishowen received the unwelcome accolade of a Norman keep, when Richard de Burgo, the 'Red Earl', built Northburg Castle at the entrance to Lough Foyle in 1305. Only the rulers of the lands of O'Neill and O'Donnell kept the foreigners at bay, from 1257 supplementing their own forces with gallowglasses (*gall-óglach*=foreign warrior), famous Scot-Norse mercenaries from the Western Isles. These and the much lighter Irish kerns (*ceithearn*=band of foot soldiers) were to play a significant part in Irish internal warfare for the next three centuries. They were hired by all sides, including the Normans and English. This meant that warring armies were often indistinguishable. These freelances were usually paid by grants of land and were often quite threatening. They were sufficiently well known to be mentioned (anachronistically) in Shakespeare's *Macbeth* (I, 2):

> The merciless Macdonwald . . . from the
> Western Isles
> Of kerns and gallowglasses is supplied . . .

The fourteenth century saw a gradual retraction of Norman possessions. Indeed, the second half of the thirteenth had seen Norman defeats in Desmond by MacCarthy in 1261, by O'Conor and O'Brien at Carrick-on-Shannon in 1270 and by Donnchad O'Brien in Thomond in 1278. Already, many of the magnates were adopting Irish ways and Irish speech, the tendency accelerated by intermarriage with children of Gaelic chieftains and the need for communication with their serfs. In 1315 a possible candidate for the high kingship arrived in the person of Edward Bruce, the brother of the hero of Bannockburn. (An offer of leadership had been made in 1262 to Haakon of Norway who, perhaps wisely, declined.) A diversionary Irish war suited Robert in his continuing struggle with Edward II of England, but there is no doubt that Edward had regal ambitions himself. He landed at Larne and after successful campaigns in Antrim and Meath was crowned 'King of Ireland' on the hill of Knocknemelan near Dundalk in 1316. To make that title substantive he needed to bring a majority of the Norman-Irish with him but his association with the unruly Donal O'Neill, king of Tír Eoghain, made this impossible. His soldiers were very effective (especially when he was joined briefly by his brother and his army) but, not having the siege engines, he failed to take Dublin. He returned north and might have held Ulster and Meath for as long as it took for supplies and reinforcements to come from Scotland, but he unwisely engaged a much larger army under de Bermingham at Faughart in 1318. He was killed after a gallant fight and his men dispersed to find their own way home. The invasion coincided with a severe famine that affected all of northern Europe and it took many years for parts of north Leinster to recover.

The Black Death (1348–9) killed about one third of the population of Ireland, and migration to England further depleted the colony. The main cause of flight and consequent shrinkage was the recovery of power by the Gaelic chiefs of the west and north (though one might argue that the latter had never lost it) and the rise of a kind of home rule movement among the premier Anglo-Irish families who now spoke English and Irish rather than French. Lionel of Clarence had failed to impose his 'lordship' and his only contribution to the stability of the colony was the utterly disregarded Statutes Of Kilkenny of 1366 (all thirty-five of them) which admitted a tripartite moral division of the population: 'Irish enemies', 'degenerate English' and the reliable inhabitants of the '*terra pacis*'. The statutory measures were directed against the middle group who wore Irish costume and spoke Irish. Even as the statutes were being enacted Gearóid Iarla, known as Gerald the Rhymer and Third Earl of Desmond (?1335–98) was busily writing such love poems as '*Mairg Adeir Olc leis na Mnáibh*' ('Speak No

Ill of Womankind').

The greater part of the Gall were by now, in the words of the seventeenth-century epigram, '*Hibernicis ipsis hiberniores*' (More Irish than the Irish). The Normans had been in some ways quite modern in their tactics and statecraft. They even had a kind of black propagandist in Giraldus Cambrensis (Gerald of Wales) (?1146–?1224) who was another son of the notorious Nesta. He became an archdeacon and acted as Prince John's chaplain when he visited Ireland. His books *Topographia Hibernica* (1184) and *Expugnatio Hibernica* (1185), though fascinating, are not at all complimentary to the native Irish and were intended as apologias for the invasion. Partly because of limited literacy, the clerical status of the writer and the linguistic excellence of the books, no formal rebuttal of 'Gerry Wales's' charges was made until a fugitive from Cromwell's Ireland, Archdeacon John Lynch, wrote *Cambrensis Aversus* in 1662. It was in this book that the useful phrase, 'more Irish than the Irish themselves', appeared; it still has its applications!

The earls of Kildare, Desmond and Ormond were now the leaders of the 'English by blood'. Of the three families, the Butlers of Ormond, lords of Tipperary, remained notably loyal to the English connection because by a royal marriage they also held lands in England (unlike the rest of the Anglo-Irish, they were Lancastrian adherents during the Wars of the Roses). The Geraldines of Kildare, because of the dominance of their leaders and their geographical proximity to the fluctuating Pale, became in the fifteenth century the most powerful family in Ireland, except for the

O'Neills, and much the most influential. The Fitzgeralds were created lords of Desmond in 1329 but rapidly became independent and Irish, while the de Burgos had long before become the Burkes of Connacht, with neither interest in nor loyalty to any English viceroys.

The kings of England from the time of Edward III (1337) to the middle of the reign of Henry VI (1453) had been fighting the Hundred Years War with France and had little time for Irish affairs. This was followed, after an interval of only two years, by the thirty-year civil Wars of the Roses. The effect of the French war was to bleed the colony of money and men. The work of Henry V's viceroy John Talbot (1414–19) in stabilising the Pale lands and facing down the Butlers was undone when he was required to be the infant Henry VI's champion in Europe after the death of the hero of Agincourt.

One not unimportant aspect of Ireland was its convenience as a bolthole for exiles or fugitives from Britain, from Donalbain in *Macbeth* ('To Ireland I . . . ') to Henry Bolingbroke. In 1459 Richard, Duke of York, fled there after his defeat by the Lancastrians at Ludlow. The Earls of Kildare and Desmond had publicly espoused the Yorkist cause but they could not resist wresting from the guest duke, who boded well to be the next king, the independence of the 'land of Ireland' under the crown. Duke Richard appointed Kildare as his deputy and returned to England, only to be killed at Wakefield in 1460.

Richard's nineteen-year-old son, Edward IV, felt himself only formally bound by the father's decrees. During his first reign (1461–70), conditions in England were sufficiently peaceful to allow him to turn his attention to Ireland and ponder the significance of his father's promises. He had appointed Earl Thomas of Desmond chief governor of Ireland in 1463 but, being temperamentally prone to rashness and persuaded that the home rule movement was reaching the point of secession, began to have doubts about this Desmond who had ignored his instructions not to continue to adopt Gaelic laws and social customs. In 1467, he sent John Tibetot, Earl of Worcester, as the king's true deputy to assert English control. Worcester was Constable of England and a noted eliminator of Lancastrian enemies. He declared Desmond and Kildare attainted and beheaded the Munster earl at Drogheda on St Valentine's Day 1468; Thomas Fitzgerald of Kildare was lucky to escape to England.

Edward IV was himself deposed in 1470 after the battle of Edgecote, and Worcester suffered the same treatment that he had doled out to many others. When Edward became king again in 1471 he found that he had no alternative but to agree to Kildare's appointment. Thus the Fitzgeralds, especially Gearóid Mór, the eighth earl, became kings of Ireland in all but name for the next sixty years. The Fitzgeralds of Desmond, by contrast, became bitter enemies of everything English and continued as a Gaelic family (they even gaelicised their name), until the family's final dissolution by Perrott and Ormond in 1583.

Political histories of the period inevitably have to concentrate on kings, earls, chiefs and battles – the sort of chronicle pilloried successfully by Sellar's and Yeatman's

1066 and All That (1930), which divided people into Good and Bad Kings and events into Good and Bad Things. True, there was continual war, especially in the Gaelic regions, and blinding, maiming, killing of hostages and treacherous breaches of parley. Yet for many, as in England during the Wars of the Roses, the war was in the next village, across the impassable bog or over the mountain. As the Anglo-Irish earls had long ago recognised, the Gaels were far from barbarian. Their orientation was towards Spain and Italy, and some chiefs of the O'Donnells and the O'Neills were as cultured as any Renaissance prince. The court poets still had their role, which required them to be a mixture of genealogist, entertainer and mage. But Gaelic conservatism and maintenance of antique systems of social life and governance were in such contrast to the more cultivated Englishry that their practices seemed offensive. The Irish preference for meeting and eating in the open air, their relatively primitive, heavily carnal and lacteal cuisine, and their costume offended the more delicately inclined English aristocracy. There did not seem to be any of the Tudor ideal of 'civility', which by the sixteenth century was largely a matter of neat farms, opulent manors, Anglican religion and respect for t'squire. The newcomers affected to see the entirely logical and ecologically efficient practice of 'booleying' as proof that Irish herdsmen were nomadic – bog-bedouins. The country of the Gaels, with its bogs, wetlands, mountains and bristling forests (to the English mind places of evil and outlawry since Saxon times), seemed entirely in keeping with the shaggy appearance of its denizens.

The Church in Ireland presented the same schismatic pattern as the country's politics. Even the primatial see was split between northern Gaels and Pale episcopalians, the English archbishop taking care to have his palace at Termonfeckin, County Louth. The practice of appointing English bishops to Gaelic sees led to absenteeism and a reversion to the practice of families having the rights to episcopal appointments, many of the incumbents illegitimate, as in the worst days before the Malachian reforms. The fifteenth century, however, witnessed a strong religious revival, headed by the Observant Franciscans and Dominicans, who built many houses, particularly in Connacht, in contrast to the decay of older foundations in Anglo-Ireland. The new spirituality was more European than English, and the more effective because it was monastic rather than secular. Atavism remained the strongest feature of the Gaelic psyche. When religion became a feature of politics, as it did from the middle of the sixteenth century on, this 'European' Catholicism was to remain a significant factor in the country's history until well into the eighteenth century.

The Wars of the Roses ended with the death at Bosworth Field of Richard III, Edward IV's brother, in 1485. The new king, Henry VII, was Welsh, and the founder of the Tudor dynasty which was to change the history of both countries. He had proved himself an astute commander against Richard and he was to prove himself an even more astute ruler in peace. His task was to heal the broken and dysfunctional country and he succeeded admirably, by a combination of diplomacy and fiscal probity, which his enemies called extortion. Yet the early years of his reign were troubled. Ireland still held to the Yorkist cause, supporting the pretenders Lambert Simnel and the more dangerous Perkin Warbeck. Henry sent Sir Edward Poynings as deputy in 1491, with the brief of hamstringing Anglo-Irish power. He arranged for a 'packed' parliament in Dublin to pass an act restoring to the Crown the appointment of all state officers, and the notorious Poynings' Law which rendered every Irish parliament powerless until its repeal in 1782, 288 years later. This act included ordinances that the boundaries of Dublin, Meath, Kildare and Louth, the four counties of the Pale (the word come from the Latin *palus*, a stake) should be marked with a double six-foot defensive ditch and, more ominously, that the chief castles of Ireland, at Dublin, Trim, Athlone, Wicklow, Carrickfergus and Green Castle (on Carlingford Lough) should have constables of English birth. The English territory thus entrenched was described in a contemporary remonstrance as 'scarcely thirty miles in length and twenty in breadth'. The same parliament caused the 'Great Earl', Garret Mór Fitzgerald, to be taken to the Tower of London but he was released in 1499 after Warbeck's execution. Henry restored him as deputy, having decided that 'since all Ireland cannot rule this man, this man must rule all Ireland'.

Now if ever was it possible for the Anglo-Irish to win some form of 'home rule'. Fitzgerald would have had support from most of the other 'English' and Gaelic chiefs, except perhaps Niall O'Neill of Tír Eoghain and the attendant lords who owed him allegiance. But the eighth earl was not tempted to break free. His own 'reign' came to an abrupt end in a local skirmish with the O'Mores of Laois in 1513. There is an appropriate irony in the fact that this last great medieval grandee should die of gunshot wounds. He was succeeded by his son Gearóid Óg, but by then Henry VII was dead and his second son was on the throne of England.

6

TUDOR QUEEN AND GAELIC PRINCE

When Henry VII's second son became king of England and
Wales in 1509, he immediately married Catherine of Aragon,
his elder brother Arthur's widow. She was six years older
than the eighteen-year-old king, who acceded to a monarchy
that was more popular and steadier than at any time since
the accession of Richard II more than 132 years previously.
His coronation was hailed by all, including the new thinkers,
Erasmus, Colet and More, and he seemed to the fearfully
cynical as rather like Machiavelli's *Il Principe*. His chief
advisor was Cardinal Wolsey, a brilliant but tactless administrator, who bore the brunt of odium for the taxation required
to finance the king's increasing extravagance and desire to
be a European rival to Charles V of Spain and Francis I of
France.

This role implied to Henry's ambitious and dynastic
mind secure continuity and he was anxious for a male heir.
But all of Catherine's children except Mary had died in
infancy and there was no precedent for a Queen Regnant.
The prospect of another civil war or rule of England by a
foreign prince was unthinkable. Under normal circumstances,

with the existence or the prospect of a healthy male heir, Anne Boleyn would probably have become the king's mistress. Catherine, however, was clearly not going to have any more children and the twenty-three year old 'Nan Bullen', niece of the Duke of Norfolk and strongly connected to the Butlers of Ormond, seemed to the anxious young king a good prospect. The result was catastrophic for England and therefore for Ireland. The situation was exacerbated by Wolsey's detestation of Gearóid Óg, the ninth Earl of Kildare, who had become lord deputy on his father's death in 1513, and the intense rivalry between the Butlers and the Fitzgeralds. Kildare spent several periods in the Tower of London while his loyalty was dissected and he finally died there in 1534.

Though not as great a statesman as his father, Gearóid Óg might under other circumstances have ruled Ireland successfully. He never recovered his health after battle wounds sustained in 1532, and by then he was Catholic deputy to a self-declared Protestant king who was head of the English church. Kildare's son, Lord Offaly ('Silken Thomas') had more dash but less diplomacy and was soon engaging a English army under Sir William Skeffington, who had been appointed deputy in 1534. Skeffington slaughtered all of the surrendered garrison of the Kildare ancestral home at Maynooth including the clerical chaplains, establishing a reputation for extreme ruthlessness that was to characterise many Tudor captains in Ireland. There would be more 'Maynooth Pardons'. Thomas, briefly tenth Earl of Kildare, was executed with his five uncles at Tyburn, all six hanged, drawn and quartered as traitors and heretics on 3 February 1537.

With the Kildare Fitzgeralds no longer a threat and Jane Seymour having produced the desired male heir, Henry felt himself able to ease the vigour of his Irish campaigns. No more anxious to embroil himself in Ireland than his daughter Elizabeth later, he settled for persuasion, and received the submission of Old English and Gaelic lords who hailed him King of Ireland, a title granted by the Dublin parliament in 1541. (The granted title was to apply to all future English monarchs. It gave rise to a legal conundrum when James II legally called himself King of Ireland after his dethronement in England in 1688.) The system of declaration of allegiance and confirmation of the aristocracies in their territories was known as 'surrender and regrant', and even the proud O'Neills in the person of Conn Bacach (?1484–1559), with a little persuasion by the deputy St Leger, crossed to England and returned as Earl of Tyrone. His eldest son Shane The Proud (*Seáan an Díomuis*), although not Conn's heir, took it upon himself to repudiate the English title and had himself declared 'The O'Neill' on his father's death. He later argued to Elizabeth herself that by Gaelic law titles were conferred on individuals merely for the period of their lives and that on Conn's death the title Earl of Tyrone would have lapsed.

By the time of Henry VIII's death in 1547, the reformation was established only in the Pale and neither of Edward VI's protectors, Somerset nor Northumberland, made much effort to convert the country as a whole; they were content with political loyalty for the time being, though it was during the rule of the latter that a strong Puritan element first made its appearance on the political scene. Edward died in 1553 and was succeeded by his elder half-sister Mary. She, unlike the next Catholic monarch, James II, proceeded cautiously in her moves to re-establish the old religion. It was not until her marriage with Philip II of Spain in 1554 that she became something of a catspaw of the Counter Reformation. She was dubbed 'Bloody Mary' because of the burnings of 'heretics', including Anglican bishops Ridley, Latimer and Cranmer, that were done in her name. It was during her reign that the first attempt at plantation as a means of keeping Ireland quiescent was attempted.

In all dealings with the Irish, English government lawyers tried where possible to have some legal basis, some small-print case, for moves against the leaders, whether in executions of traitors or confiscations of their lands, the one often giving the excuse for the other. In 1557 the territories of Laois and Offaly were shired as Queen's County and King's County. The Offaly territory had been proscribed as belonging to the 'traitor' Silken Thomas and a distant connection with the house of Mortimer served the lawyers with sufficient lien to seize the land of the O'Mores. Two-thirds of the land was confiscated and, although the dispossessed O'Connors and O'Mores continued to fight guerilla wars for the next half-century, by 1603 the garrison settlements of Maryborough and Philipstown were well-established.

Elizabeth I, who succeeded to the English throne in

1558, was very much her grandfather's daughter, reluctant to spend money unnecessarily, and like her father she would have preferred to pacify Ireland by negotiation rather than conquest. Until her accession she had lived a precarious existence, declared illegitimate by her father, cold-shouldered and later imprisoned by her Catholic half-sister, and was a much more skilled politician than either. The Irishman who was to be her greatest adversary had been fostered in England by Sir Henry Sidney, the lord deputy who, with a fine instinct, realised that the nine-year-old Hugh was the significant O'Neill. The boy had been reared in the new religion and was perfectly at home in the English court. It was when he returned to Ireland at the age of eighteen in 1568 that the atavistic desire to rule became too strong. He was, with occasional lapses, as astute and as patient as the queen and seriously upset her ambition to solve swiftly and once for all the Irish question.

The O'Neills in their Ulster fastnesses were the premier Gaelic family, and showed the classical pattern of internal dissension and fierce enmity with rivals. Shane the Proud was a notorious harrier of the O'Donnells and the O'Neills of east Ulster, and he was sworn enemy to the Scots-Irish MacDonnells. Indeed he attacked at one time or another all the territories that touched his own land. Elizabeth, with remarkable patience, allowed him to rule as Earl of Tyrone but he had gathered too many enemies over the years. It was the MacDonnells who finally murdered him in 1567, while he was a guest at a feast, in revenge for his treatment of them and their leader Sorley Boy (Somhairle Buí). Sorley Boy

MacDonnell was to have experience of the cruelty of Elizabethan officials in 1575, having to watch from Tor Head in north Antrim the massacre – on the orders of the Earl of Essex – of his wife and children on Rathlin Island where they had been sent for safety. Walter Devereux, first Earl of Essex, had come to Ireland to win a name, money and power; he was not notably successful and won a name for ruthlessness instead.

He and other talented but ruthless Englishmen, who saw in Ireland a chance for a career, were often at odds with Elizabeth, not about the means they used to punish the non-compliers with English plans for settlement, but rather because they recommended a much more radical solution. The words 'extirpation' and 'genocide' were not used then, but they would have liked to rub out the genealogical map of Ireland and start afresh. It was the mindset of the Spanish conquistadores and many other military colonists, who found aboriginal inhabitants an inconvenience. They combined a complete disregard of the 'uncivil' Gaels with a dislike of the Catholicism of the Old English. In this respect Queen Elizabeth was something more compassionate, but dreaded the possibility that Ireland would be the means of the Counter Reformation reconquering England by the back door.

In the decade 1573–83 there were risings in Munster, Queen's and King's Counties and Wicklow which achieved little. All, but especially the outbreaks in the southwest, were put down with exemplary savagery, by Lord Deputy Grey de Wilton and by Perrott, Ormond and Carew. There were few battles, the campaign rather consisting of sieges and massacres, including the killing in 1580 at Smerwick near Ballyferriter in the Dingle peninsula of a mixed force of seven hundred Spaniards and Italians sent by Pope Gregory XIII and Philip II of Spain. The Lord Deputy's deputy was the young Walter Raleigh and his extremism on that occasion was not at all unwelcome to the queen, whose favourite he rapidly became. He was one of the first to benefit from the Munster plantation which followed the desolation of Desmond. 210,000 acres of good land was confiscated – 'relinquished' by the attainted earl and his supporters. Raleigh managed to acquire 40,000 acres, and 4,000 English settlers were established in Cork, Limerick and Tipperary. The purpose, as in the Marian plantations in Laois/Offaly, was to have a solid body of English Protestant inhabitants in what had been Catholic and essentially anti-English land.

The queen was perfectly happy to have rebels slaughtered, but in days of relative peace she preferred inaction to the logic of such advisers as Surrey in her father's time and Sussex in her own. Neither monarch had the stomach nor the means to attempt the obliteration of the uncivilised, who were now also heretics. The country of Ireland was in the process of colonisation but in fact the rate of application was very slow. Most of the anti-clerical, anti-Catholic measures were not enforced and it was not until the reign of Queen Anne (1702–14) that Catholic leadership was rendered totally ineffective. The plantation of Ulster, the Cromwellian settlement, the Jacobite war – none of these were ultimately successful. Elizabeth has a place in the Irish demonology not far below that of Oliver Cromwell but she was, considering the practices of the time, considerably less absolute than Anne (or her advisers) and in an odd way more sympathetic to the Irish than, say, George III. The extremes of her deputies who were, as it seemed to them, merely consolidating their investments, were not always justly visited on her – and she seems to have had a soft spot for Hugh O'Neill.

This Earl of Tyrone must have been a man of great charm, since he ran diplomatic rings round the second Earl of Essex and was treated with respect and clemency by his vanquisher Mountjoy and the new king. He gave the impression of being Lord Facing-both-Ways, at once the loyal holder of regranted titles, Baron Dungannon in 1568 and Earl of Tyrone in 1585, and yet the chieftain of the oldest and strongest family in Gaelic Ireland. He had led a cavalry troop against the Desmonds in 1569 but had assumed the title 'The O'Neill' at the prehistoric inauguration stone at Tullyhogue near Cookstown in 1595, and effectively thrown the gauntlet down at Elizabeth's feet. He understood the English mind as few Irishmen of the time did, but old instincts and the realisation that a palatinate in Ulster was achievable with himself as leader caused him to seek confrontation with, if not the queen, her officials. He probably realised that the personal accommodation that he had made with Elizabeth might, like Gaelic chieftainship, end either at her death or at his. At that period in history, England's *realpolitik* required of its neighbours either a treaty based on stability or that country's subjugation.

Ireland could not of its nature by Tudor definition be classed as stable and sooner or later, therefore, the country would have to be quieted.

O'Neill was a fine captain who had learned the value of the new weapons of war, especially cannon and explosives, and he was able to rally great support from the other chieftains, even from his hereditary enemies, the O'Donnells, by suggesting that any war against England would be a religious one. Elizabeth reluctantly declared him a traitor and sent a number of commanders against him. He defeated Sir John Norris at Clontibret on 13 June 1595 and would have routed his army except that he ran out of shot. Three years later at the Yellow Ford, near Armagh, the combined armies of O'Neill, Red Hugh O'Donnell (who received the accolade of a Disney movie, *The Fighting Prince of Donegal*) and Hugh Maguire of Fermanagh inflicted on Sir Henry Bagenal the severest defeat ever sustained by an English army in Ireland. O'Neill was Bagenal's brother-in-law since his elopement with Bagenal's sister Mabel in 1591. The political misalliance, the thirty years' difference in age, an unpaid dowry and the husband's infidelities meant that the marriage was unhappy, and Bagenal, who had once been O'Neill's brother-in-arms, became his implacable enemy. Mabel had died in 1596 and her brother was killed at the Yellow Ford.

O'Neill dealt with the next Tudor champion even more conclusively: Robert Devereux, second Earl of Essex and son of the butcher of Rathlin, was humiliated at Aclint on the Louth-Monaghan border when his army of 20,000 troops was dismissed, at the start of a truce engineered by a supremely confident Tyrone. It was the start of a downward spiral which would lead to Essex's disgrace and death in 1601. Essex's replacement as lord deputy was to be O'Neill's nemesis. Charles Blount, Lord Mountjoy, was a much better strategist and commanded a much better equipped army than O'Neill. His policy was a kind of summary of Tudor captains' tactics with destruction of property and burning of crops added to the usual slaughter of all opponents. His deliberate desecration of the Tullyhogue stone and the burning of Dungannon in 1602 were effective in driving O'Neill out of Ulster and making his struggle a countrywide crusade. Help was promised by Philip III of Spain, but when del Águila's force arrived it landed at the entirely inappropriate port of Kinsale.

O'Neill, persuaded by the flamboyant O'Donnell, marched through an Ireland in the grip of a bitter winter and succeeded in getting between Mountjoy and his supply line to Cork. The most appropriate tactic was to starve the superior English army into submission but, as ever, the impatient Irish armies had neither stomach nor proper equipment for a siege. The attrition did not suit the Spaniards either, and against his will and better judgement O'Neill, whose successes had been achieved mainly by ambush and mobility, consented to a formal battle. The opposing forces met on the morning of Christmas Eve, 1601. It was all over in three hours and Gaelic Ireland had received its death blow. O'Neill retreated north again and Red Hugh left for Spain with the remnants of del Águila's army and was received with some cordiality by the king. But no further help was forthcoming. The fighting prince of Donegal died on 10 September 1602 in Simancas, probably poisoned by James Blake, an agent of his old enemy Sir George Carew.

O'Neill finally surrendered to Mountjoy in March 1603, unaware that Elizabeth had died. James I received him and Rory O'Donnell, Red Hugh's younger brother, and reinstated them both, Rory becoming Earl of Tyrconnell. Mountjoy had proved a worthy enemy and now became a friend at court, travelling with them on the ship *Tramontana* that took him from Ireland for the last time, no doubt to his intense relief. His death in 1606 was one of the reasons for what became known as the 'Flight of the Earls'. O'Neill might have held on to his possessions, but both Irish and English were moving against him. Mountjoy's replacement, Chichester, was determined on the anglicisation of Ulster, a process he hoped might be slow and relatively gentle. His colleague Sir John Davies had other ideas and offered Ireland to James 'as a fruitful Canaan'. This promised land would require certain preparations before the latter-day Israelites could take possession; these included the extirpation of the Gaelic system and the parcelling out of the escheated lands to the deserving, the civilised and the religiously and politically loyal.

O'Donnell shared the somewhat manic temperament of his elder brother and neither rested content with the remarkably generous settlement that the king had granted nor had the courage and will effectively to oppose it. He engaged in a number of conspiracies without result and he had to suffer the indignity of good O'Donnell lands being given away. Sir Cahir O'Doherty, then a government favourite, had been granted the territory of Inishowen and his enemy kinsman, Niall Garbh O'Donnell, given the most fertile acres in Donegal, the eastern territory around Lifford. His plotting was more than just an embarrassment to Tyrone. His old enemies, the O'Cahans, had successfully petitioned James I for a hearing about disputed territory in north Derry, and both O'Neill and Donal O'Cahan had been summoned to Westminster.

Meanwhile, the chief of Fermanagh, Cuchonnacht Maguire, had no illusions about the future of Gaelic Ulster after Kinsale. He commissioned a Breton vessel (financed by Philip III with O'Neill's son Henry as agent) which appeared at Rathmullen on the west shore of Lough Swilly in Donegal in the late August of 1607. O'Donnell, Maguire and a numerologically significant total of ninety-nine other Ulster lords began making preparations for embarkation. O'Neill was in Meath presiding at court sessions with Chichester when he heard the news. In sudden haste he moved his household from Dungannon and joined the ship in Rathmullen. She slipped out on 4 September and discharged her noble cargo in the Spanish Netherlands, whence they made the agonisingly slow overland journey to Rome. Ugo, Conte di Tirone, was received kindly by Pope Paul V and lived until 1616 as a pensionary of the Spanish king.

He died, aged sixty-six, of 'melancholy', having failed in his rationalised purpose for exile: the better organisation of resistance to the British in Ireland. Philip III was scholarly, religious and scanting of his political responsibilities, and did not fully realise that the great days of his country were over. There would be no Spanish-led Counter Reformation in England or Ireland; Philip knew in his heart that its religious drive was compromised badly by the political rivalries of France, Rome and his own country. He probably felt that he had fulfilled his moral obligation by allowing O'Neill to live in comfortable exile.

The country O'Neill left was still mainly in the hands of Catholics, though its character had changed in the hundred years since Henry VIII's accession; the next hundred years was to change it utterly. The creaming off of Irish aristocracy that began with his flight was to continue until with the spreading of grey wings upon the tide the Wild Geese should leave Catholic Ireland utterly leaderless and require them to devise new systems of survival and regeneration. Older historians have tried to decry the word 'flight' but the description holds even in its precipitancy. O'Neill might have survived and shaped a new Ulster but his temper was against such accommodation as he would have been required to make. He remains a fascinating if persistently enigmatic figure, without doubt a Gaelic prince and certainly the last of his kind.

7

Planter, Gael, Jacobite

The Stuarts who ruled Britain for seventy years in the seventeenth century were no more friendly to the Old Irish than the Tudors; any clemency shown, and it was slight and intended to be advantageous to the Crown, was to the Catholic Old English. Even if James II had been victorious in his part of the war of the Three Kings (known locally as *cogadh an dá rí*), a distinct possibility at the beginning of 1690, Ireland would have been ruled by a Catholic aristocracy under a Catholic replica of Charles I. As it was, his defeat meant that the Irish question was more or less settled for over a hundred years. The need to accept or obliterate the religion of the Catholic Irish was never faced and the problem was not dead but dormant.

The first Stuart king of England was the most decisive, largely because his title was secure and he inherited a loyal country from Elizabeth. His Presbyterian upbringing clashed with his extreme views of royalty, as his treatise *True Law of Free Monarchies* (1598), written while he was James VI of Scotland, affirmed, respeaking the distinctly unCalvinistic doctrine of the divine right of kings. This belief, passed on to his less astute son, and mixed in his case with a cavalier attitude to the growing power of Puritanism, were to lead to a catastrophic civil clash in which politics and religion were horribly mixed.

James's early experience made him confident in dealing with the Scots-Irish of Ulster, and they trusted him as none of the other monarchs of his line. The departure of the Gaelic earls made a large area in west, central and south Ulster available for redistribution. The province had been shired by 1580, and English county structures imposed upon 'alien and uncivil' lands. The lands of Armagh, Fermanagh, Cavan and Donegal were to be marked out in lots that varied from 1,000 to 3,000 acres and granted to 'undertakers', 'servitors' (ex-servicemen) and compliant natives. The Scots were assigned lands in north and east Tyrone, south Donegal and parts of Fermanagh, but their later strength was to be in Antrim and Down, their numbers increasing as the century advanced. James had approved the 'private' plantations established there and saw the advantages of using Lowland Scot stock as planters elsewhere in the unruly province.

Other portions were set aside for English, the Church and Elizabeth's 'civilising' university of the Holy Trinity (founded in 1592). The county of Coleraine was extended to include the barony of Loughinsholin, which gave it access to the Lough Neagh foreshore, a portion of old O'Donnell land on the west bank of the Foyle and an encroachment on County Antrim, east of the Bann. The parcel was granted to the city of London and its livery companies and its name changed to London-derry. The name, even in its unhyphenated form, was never acceptable to the Old Irish and even today its use is entirely political.

The settlement of Derry had been acquired in 1600 by Sir Henry Docwra and he had as protégé the young lord of Inishowen, Sir Cahir O'Doherty, whom he hoped would be a more manageable, if lesser version of Tyrone. In 1606, Docwra sold his interests in the town and environs to George Paulett, who had no use for the fiery lordling. They quarrelled publicly in 1608 – Paulett struck him in an argument over property – and O'Doherty, with the support of O'Hanlons and Sweeneys, organised an uprising from his castle at Burt, eight miles from the small city. Paulett died in O'Doherty's attack on the city but O'Doherty himself was killed in a skirmish near Kilmacrenan in Donegal. O'Doherty had been foreman of the jury that, in 1607, condemned the flown earls as traitors; now, in the year of his twenty-first birthday, his head was spiked above Newgate next to Christ Church.

He had left the tiny city of Derry in ruins and the London merchants reluctantly accepted their commission to fortify it and develop it commercially. Its walls were completed in 1618 but the town was vulnerable to attack from the river and the surrounding hills were much higher than the little acropolis on which it was built. The building was beset by corruption, bureaucracy and lack of enthusiasm in the undertakers, and they found themselves severely fined by Charles I's minister Wentworth for various contraventions of the charter, including sloth and the use of native labour. The territory of Inishowen, in forfeit since O'Doherty ('that audacious traitor') had shown how ineffective an English education could be, was granted to a suitably grateful Chichester.

The Ulster plantation succeeded better than any previous initiatives but it did not achieve its purpose of removing the disloyal natives. Parcels of land grant were based upon the Irish acre which was calculated, not by the extent of the property, but by its yield. Since the land under the old dispensation was, in general, not very productive, the result was that the grants were much larger than had been intended. 'Balliboes' (baile bó='pasturage') and 'ballybetaghs' (baile biatiagh='food-producing land'), the plantation units, showed great variations, say between the land of the Laggan between Tyrone and Donegal, the best land in west Ulster, and the bogs and bare hills of the Sperrins. Native tenants were not only encouraged but were found to be necessary for good husbandry, and the dispossessed often found themselves working on land that once was theirs. Far from 'anglicisation' or even 'colonisation', there had been established a province with two mutually antagonistic populations.

In other plantation areas, Munster, Wexford, Leitrim, Longford, King's County, Queen's County, some of the government's intentions were carried out, but in general the schemes attracted not the hoped-for sober and industrious but the rogues and opportunists, 'discarded unjust serving-men, younger sons to younger brothers, revolted tapsters and ostlers trade-fallen, the cankers of a calm world and a long peace'. 'Overcrowding' and limited possibilities for wealth acquisition characterised the age of Elizabeth (and were later to be just as typical of Jacobean Britain). America was the exploiters' promised land but Ireland was a more convenient source of profit. Some planters used plantations as an apprenticeship for the real pickings in Virginia and many sold their portions soon after incorporation. In the early plantations land began to be reacquired by those who had lost it, rendering the original purpose null.

Ulster, by comparison, could be regarded as a success. There the land was to the adventurers' eyes virgin and full of possibilities, and they could salve their commercial consciences with the flattering unction that they were bringing the true religion and were scourges of the hated popery. Conversion of the Catholics was, in fact, the last thing they wanted. (In the Scots settlement, where Presbyterianism thrived, they hated the recusants but would certainly not have trusted any converts.) Towns appeared; roads were made, forests cleared and bogs drained. A lot of money was made by the exploitation of Ulster's natural resources, and timber was shipped out in great amounts. The drumlin lands proved suitable for flax and linen; wool, cattle and butter became the basis for a thriving export trade. Churches and meeting houses were built and, mainly, in the west, Gaelic was learnt. A remarkable amount of intermarriage took place and there was a tolerable peace.

James I died on 27 March 1625, to be succeeded by his second son Charles I. The new king was no more assiduous than his father in insisting upon the imposition of absolute reformation ideals upon the Catholic Irish but his ambitions, the character of his advisers and his own personality led inevitably to the clashes with Calvinistic Scotland, with his own parliament and with a growing democratic movement that was associated with, if not coextensive with, English Puritanism. Charles dismissed parliament in 1629 and ruled for the next eleven years without it, financing his wars with arbitrary taxes. His lord deputy Wentworth, appointed in 1632, enforced Archbishop Laud's anti-Puritanism on the Irish church, alienated the New English with his insistence upon the king's absolute authority in England and collected a lot of money for his royal master from the Old Catholics in return for promised 'Graces', which in practice meant some little relief from religious debility. Wentworth (Earl of Strafford from 1649) managed to offend everyone in Ireland. In pursuance of Laud's canon that, even abroad, the king's subjects should not attend 'Calvinistic' services, he imposed the 'Black Oath' in 1639 on Scots in Ulster to forswear the covenant taken in Edinburgh the previous year.

Laud's Scots initiative in imposing Anglicanism on Scotland led to the 'Bishops' War' that Charles lost, and Laud's own execution in 1640. The king was forced to recall a largely unRoyalist parliament and Strafford's career ended, as did Laud's, with execution on a bill of attainder on 12 May 1641. The Catholic landowners in Ireland, both Old English and Old Irish, sensing that dissensions in Britain might give them an opportunity, decided to emulate the Scots and show some armed force, even using the king's name in their move against the largely parliamentarian rule in Dublin. Plans to seize Dublin Castle were discovered on 22 October the eve of the appointed day, but the risings in

Ulster under Sir Phelim O'Neill and in Leinster led by Sir Rory O'More were initially successful. The dispossessed Irish turned on their masters. 2,000 Protestant settlers were killed, while many thousands more were stripped, dispossessed and 'driven into the waste'. The massacre marked the beginnings of a struggle of extreme complexity that involved, in varying permutations, the dispossessed Irish, the many Old Irish who still retained their lands, the Old English, the New English, the Ulster Scots, English and Scots armies of king and parliament, the churches and Archbishop Rinuccini, the representative of the Counter Reformation. The conflict would not end until the country was settled by the New Model Army. Its leaders, Oliver Cromwell, his son Henry, his son-in-law, Henry Ireton, and Edmund Ludlow, imposed a near-final solution as there had been no real opposition since the early death of the only efficient military leader, Owen Roe O'Neill (?1590–1649). His was the major military success of the eleven-year struggle, when he defeated the Scots under Robert Monro at Benburb, but his successor, Bishop Heber MacMahon, was no general. He was captured after a defeat near Letterkenny and was executed in Enniskillen on 17 September 1650.

The year 1641 is the remembered year for Ulster Protestants, joining Pearl Harbour, Armenia, the Famine and more recently Bosnia as examples of particular infamy. The numbers of Protestant dead were grossly exaggerated and the distortion has been incorporated in all Protestant histories since. The memory of a similar massacre of large numbers of Catholics at Island Magee in County Antrim the following January, when Monro's Scots killed children with the cry, 'Nits make lice', has not lasted. The propaganda was so effective that memories of much more widespread killings by the parliamentary armies are not so sharp. By modern standards of 'ethnic cleansing', even Cromwell's 'punishments' were negligible and it is clear with hindsight that it was the 'push from below' of the dispossessed which changed the nature of Phelim O'Neill's and Rory O'More's 'loyal rising'.

Cromwell's commonwealth lasted ten years and by then English republicanism had changed its nature. The militaristic nature of Britain at the time of death of its king required some non-royal form of government, and Cromwell's establishment of a peaceful England allowed time for the country's conservatism to reassert itself. The Puritans in armour were given leave to attack the ancient institutions which were really repositories of Catholicism, whether Roman or Anglican, and in time exhausted their rage. In this sense, Cromwell served England well and his memory probably did not deserve the exhumation and gibbetting of his body that occurred when the monarchy was restored in the person of Charles II in 1660. His reputation was not that of an extremist at home, but he was an intensely religious man and the clue to all of his actions is that he was ever-convinced of the righteousness of his course.

In Ireland he is the great Satan who slaughtered Drogheda, Wexford and Clonmel and completed the Tudor transfer of land from Irish to British proprietors. The Irish who were innocent of involvement in the war still had their lands confiscated, but they were conceded small estates west of the

Shannon, such as should have neither coastal nor riparian access. 34,000 soldiers were allowed to leave the country with their officers and there was some selling of native Irish into West Indian slavery. The poor were, in general, allowed to continue undisturbed being poor. The Catholic-held lands in the twenty-six counties that were left when those of Connacht, with Clare, were subtracted were sold or assigned to pay for the war. Parliamentary veterans were granted land consonant with their ranks and services, and many sold their rights. The country, depopulated by famine, war and emigration, survived the 1650s and, though rooting out of Catholicism was part of Cromwell's plan, the religious persecution was not as efficient nor as wholehearted as might have been expected. Evangelisation was hampered by language difficulties and, though much lower than Laud might have wished, the episcopalian Church of Ireland was not Cromwellian.

The Restoration changed little. James Butler, Duke of Ormond, head of the oldest Royalist family in Ireland, was made lord lieutenant in 1661 and disappointed the dispossessed Catholics by his recommendation that the Cromwellian settlement should remain virtually untouched. He was disappointed himself but he feared the kind of Protestant backlash that led in England to the allegations in 1678 of a 'Popish Plot' and the execution of St Oliver Plunkett, Archbishop of Armagh, in Ireland. That incident and the death of Peter Talbot, Archbishop of Dublin, in prison, were the only notable examples of religious intolerance during an otherwise tolerant reign. Relaxation was evidenced in the return of Catholic schoolmasters and the flourishing of Franciscan foundations. The relative tolerance in religion had its counterpart politically as well. Charles II's reign was noted for the existence of 'tories' (*tóraí*=hunter, bandit) and 'rapparees' (*rapaire*=half-pike, highwayman) who were not so much guerrillas as independent outlaw chieftains who lived 'like the old Robin Hood of England'. Probably the most famous of these was Count Redmond O'Hanlon, who 'ruled' parts of Tyrone and Armagh before his execution in 1681.

The death of Charles (as a Catholic) in 1685 and the accession of his admiral brother James changed the picture dramatically. James II was not the avenging Papist tyrant that Whig historians have painted him. He had become a Catholic on the death of his first wife Anne Hyde in 1671 and his second marriage was to Mary, the daughter of the Italian Duke of Modena. He had left England during the Popish Plots riots in 1679 and his accession upset the instinctively anti-Catholic English establishment. Their fears increased when the queen, after losing five children in early childhood, in 1688 bore James a son who survived to become James III in the eyes of the Jacobites and the 'Old Pretender' to everyone else before 1745. Lord Danby, the Whig leader who had arranged the marriage of the king's daughter with William of Orange, now sent for his protégé, and James II fled to France. That he did so was of considerable relief to his enemies, since not even they could contemplate regicide of a son as well. After a period of consultation at the court of Louis XIV, where he was well received, he landed in

Kinsale in March 1689. He came as King of Ireland with a small French army. Louis needed all his strength to continue the war against the Grand Alliance of Spain, Britain, Holland, Bavaria, Austria and Pope Innocent XI. Whatever about James's little corner of it, the main war was clearly not about anybody's true faith.

James's deputy, Richard Talbot, Earl of Tyrconnell, was able to provide him with a Catholic parliament and a Catholic army which, though it failed to shake the Ulster-Scots yeomanry and could not lift the siege of Derry, was regarded as a match for the Protestant and English armies. The early months of 1690 seemed bleak for William III (declared joint monarch with Mary in February 1689). His support in England was weak, as the Tory majority was expecting another Restoration. His only hope was success in Ireland and, as the protagonists saw it, the struggle was not so much against the Stuart king or for the English colonists in Ireland as a fight to avoid domination by France and to save Protestantism in Europe. It was to be the last decisive stand against the Counter Reformation and it was successful. At Derry, Aughrim, Enniskillen and the Boyne, to use the Orange chant which makes up in euphony what it lacks in chronological sequence, 'our freedom, religion and laws' were safeguarded forever. It was as 'near-run' a thing as Waterloo, especially at Aughrim, but Ginkel's defeat of the French-Irish army settled the matter and Irish Ireland entered a cryonic state from which the waking was to be unconscionably slow and painful. After 'Aughrim's great disaster' more than a hundred years of apparent suspended animation had to be suffered before a new Ireland should, in the words of one of her best midwives, be 'a nation once again.'

8

'The Very Definition of Slavery'

Jonathan Swift, whose eighteenth-century Dublin exile as
Dean of St Patrick's Cathedral turned him into a vociferous
champion of Irish autonomy ('Fair Liberty was all his cry'),
wrote in 1720 as part of his famous 'Drapier' pamphlet
agitation, 'Government without the consent of the governed
is the very definition of slavery.' He applied it to an
Ascendancy parliament effectively hamstrung by the old
Poynings' Law of 1494 and by the act known as the 'Sixth
of George I'. This measure, passed in 1720, gave Westminster
the right to legislate for Ireland. The objections of the
landowning minority were muted, mainly because English
governments allowed a public sense of local power. It was
only when such important matters as the army and finance
were in question that their real powerlessness became
apparent. There was little they could do, for example, about
Britain's export restrictions which, from 1699, effectively
ruined the Irish wool trade.

The Drapier agitation was, in fact, effective – William
Wood's licence to mint a new Irish coinage was withdrawn
– but this small victory was an exception. The Dublin

parliament was mainly a house for the ratification of the elaborate system of oligarchy maintenance, with its pensions, preferments and political jobbery. Effective power in Ireland was sited in Dublin Castle and in the person of the Lord Lieutenant. The country which the Dublin parliament undertook to legislate for had in 1690 a population of something over two million, which rose, however, after a 'peaceful' century to near five million by 1800. Of these 75 per cent were Catholics who after the end of the Williamite war owned 14 per cent of the land. This figure was further whittled down by effective penal laws, so that by 1778 barely one-twentieth of Irish land was in Catholic hands.

The treaty concluded by Ginkel on William III's behalf was not illiberal. Catholics were to be given the same religious liberty they had enjoyed under Charles II or as were consistent 'with the laws of Ireland' (a phrase which left a crack through which later penal laws might seep). The treaty, which had its element of Victorian melodrama in a 'missing clause', was rejected by the Irish parliament, which was to maintain a resolutely anti-Catholic mien throughout the eighteenth century, yielding concessions with great reluctance and only when strongly pressurised by Britain. Even the 'patriots', who were the forensic glory of what was later called 'Grattan's Parliament', were largely anti-Papist. Many of the 'volunteers', the local militias which came into existence at the time of the American Revolutionary War and were characterised as much by sartorial elegance as by military muscle, were specifically anti-Catholic. A flamboyant and intermittent emancipationist like Frederick Hervey,

Earl of Bristol and Bishop of (rich) Derry, found that his support of the majority angered his commander-in-chief, the Earl of Charlemont, and resulted in his military and political power being severely circumscribed.

William III's position was more secure than he may have believed, but when the Westminster parliament proved nearly as adamantly anti-Catholic as their brothers in Chichester House he acquiesced in the anti-popery laws that were begun in his reign. He did what he could to mitigate the severity of their application at home but for all his tolerance there was little he could do or was prepared to try against the entrenched Protestantism of Ireland. After Limerick the country lost most of its remaining Catholic aristocracy and its Jacobite army. Sarsfield led 11,000 officers and men into exile to join the 5,000 who were already members of the Irish Brigade in France. Yet two million alienated people, however leaderless and disaffected, could neither be trusted nor empowered. An earlier, more ruthless age might (some say did) have opted for genocide. William Allingham's 'Antrim Presbyterian' in *Laurence Bloomfield in Ireland* spoke for many Anglicans too when he said, 'Far too briefly Cromwell ruled'. After 1690, however, sensibilities were becoming marginally more delicate and such a solution, though fitting for the American Indian and the native Tasmanian in the next century, did not quite square with ideals of Enlightenment which were then beginning to burgeon. Besides, the large population of peasants was needed to work the escheated lands.

The measures taken were rather like those enacted

against members of minority faiths in France and Spain, but there dissenters represented tiny minorities. In Ireland, however, the established church ministered to only one-sixth of the population but took tithes from everyone. (Catholics and Presbyterians continued to resent this tax until its abatement in 1836.) In 1719, a Toleration Act exempted Protestant dissenters from the religious disabilities that they had formerly shared with Catholics but they were still unable to play a full part in public life because of the Test Act of 1704. This disability was to play a decisive part in the history of south and east Ulster throughout the eighteenth century and was the main cause of a purely contingent loyalty to Britain from the 1860s to the present day. The main purpose of the penal laws was formally to exclude Catholics from participation in public life and to prevent their owning land. There were specifically anti-confessional measures but these fell into abeyance after about a decade.

The main 'anti-Popery' enactments began in 1695, with prohibitions on Catholics from educating their children at home or abroad, bearing arms, joining the army or owning a horse worth more than £5. (No Catholic could refuse to sell his horse for that price.). In 1697 'all papists exercising ecclesiastical jurisdiction and all regulars of the popish clergy' were given nine months to leave the kingdom. From 1704 Catholics were restricted from buying land or holding leases for longer than thirty-one years. On the death of a Catholic father all the sons (or if necessary daughters) were given equal shares, though the eldest could inherit if he conformed to the established church. Even more miserably unjust was the right given to even distant conforming cousins to bring a 'discovery suit' and claim the land from the papist owner. A test act required all holders of public office to take the Anglican communion. All professions except medicine were closed to non-Anglicans and inevitably a large numbers of lawyers and members of other professions rushed to conform. A majority of the remaining Catholic landlords also took the necessary oaths.

By these means the main Ascendancy intentions were achieved: most Catholics were excluded from landowning and no Catholics had political representation. (The last of the penal enactments was made in 1728, when Catholics were disenfranchised.) By the reign of George I (1714–27) it was possible to say that 'the law does not suppose any such person to exist as an Irish Roman Catholic.' Only zealots persisted in the purely religious prohibitions after an early period of rigid enforcement. There were professional priest catchers and occasional suggestions that unregistered priests should be branded or castrated. These were merely an embarrassment to the Castle and even the Protestant Irish establishment were in general unenthusiastic. Greed rather than conviction seems to have been the motive for most of the legislation. The horror stories of the Penal Days (always in upper-case), that like the Famine lore of the next century provided later generations (mainly in exile) with an emotional store of long-lasting anti-British feeling, described exceptions rather than norms. There were urban churches in existence by the 1720s although Belfast's first 'Mass-house' in Chapel Lane was not built till 1783. This, like Derry's first church the Long Tower, built a year later, was supported by subscriptions from all creeds including Anglicans. It was in the years of unofficial tolerance that the designation 'chapel' for a place of Catholic worship, which lasted in colloquial language until comparatively recent times, was first used, since only Anglican edifices could be called 'churches'. Priests wore ordinary dress and were known socially as 'Mister' rather than 'Father'. In the country, private houses, barns or shelters were used for the celebration of Mass and Benediction but much depended upon the attitude of the local landlord. This meant that in the north the building of chapels was practically unknown until the last quarter of the eighteenth century. The phenomenon, observable until the mid-1950s, that the Catholic church was usually sited several miles beyond the boundaries of Ulster towns is a reminder of this grudging tolerance.

As the century progressed, a number of urban Catholics, prevented from other outlets for their talents, prospered in trade. This was true mainly of the larger towns like Limerick, Waterford and Cork where Catholic tradespeople grew to be a majority – and, of course, Dublin, though here they remained a minority only. Even in Derry, Belfast, Newry and Armagh there was a measurable Catholic bourgeoisie. They tended to be conservative, publicly loyal to the British crown (in the words of Charles O'Conor of Belanagare, the first modern Catholic leader, 'good Protestants in politics') and content to await what amelioration of their condition time would bring. In parts of Connacht and Munster, where remoteness made enforcement of complicated laws difficult anyway, there were still Catholic landlords. The descendants of some of these who on the wilder shores of the Atlantic supplemented their income with the proceeds of a smuggling economy with France and Spain were to play significant roles in nineteenth-century politics, notably Daniel O'Connell from Derrynane in Kerry, while others like George Moore and Edward Martyn had more cultural parts to play.

A majority of the Catholic population was unaffected by laws of any kind. They survived by their labour and the subsistence of their tiny holdings. There is a painful irony in Swift's applying to burghers who were at the very least comfortably off his definition of slavery, when his cathedral was surrounded by slums of an appalling condition. The lowest level of the agricultural population, the cottiers and *spailpíní* (seasonal labourers), were marginally more healthy than the town dwellers but tuberculosis and smallpox were rife. Their diet was quite well balanced: potatoes, milk, butter, bacon and cheese combined with tubers and a more nourishing potato than the 'lumper', which was universally adopted towards the end of the century because of its higher yield, produced a peasantry famous for its capacity for labour. They were susceptible to regularly recurring famines: the early years of the 1740s were a kind of ominous dress rehearsal for the terrible visitation a hundred years later. In both cases, severe frost removed the subsistence upon which a class without reserves depended; potatoes rotted and famine fever claimed as many as did hunger. Its effects were not as apocalyptic as in the Great Famine since the numbers involved were only a quarter of the 1840s population and they were less dependent upon the potato.

The practice of religion by the Catholic Irish was not greatly different from that of a hundred and fifty years earlier. Side by side with normal sacramental practice, which in the early part of the century was necessarily gappy because of the ratio of approved priests to souls and the geographical extent of many parishes subsisting without church buildings, were older cultish practices, associated with pilgrimages and 'patterns' (the word comes from 'patron'), holy wells and 'relics'. Wakes were as festive as weddings and folklore as potent as theology. Since in normal years subsistence varied from possible to easy, and expectations about the comfort of living conditions were low, marriages were early and, allowing for infant deaths, prolific. 'Cabins' without windows, often without chimneys, were not difficult to build especially since co-operation (the Irish word was *meitheal*)meant that there was always plenty of free (and skilful) labour available. The cinematically and theatrically preserved reputation of the Irish 'broths' of boys and winsome colleens, who would sing, dance, drink and break heads with shillelaghs at faction-fights, all with equal zest, had its origin at this time.

The hovels of the poor were in stark contrast to the grandeur of the 'Big Houses' that were built as much to establish the contrast as to satisfy social requirements and often were not consonant with the fiscal situations of their owners. The need of colonial masters to demonstrate their hegemony over 'natives' and their moral independence from the old country in fabric seems to have been instinctive. It was to mean that Georgian Dublin, created from the 1770s on, was startlingly elegant but, compared with the generally debased state of the country, grotesquely inappropriate, 'as your pearl in your foul oyster'. The urban culture which thanks to Smock Alley and Crow Street made Dublin the theatrical peer of London, and Fishamble Street the scene of the first performance of Handel's *Messiah*, conducted by the composer on 13 April 1742, had equivalences in the country and small towns. There were theatres in most large-sized towns and they were supplied partly by local repertories but mainly by touring companies. Mrs Siddons's performance in *The Unhappy Marriage* in 1785 had so strong an effect on such of Belfast's 20,000 inhabitants as attended that many ladies fainted.

When Thomas Davis began writing for the *Nation* in 1842 he calculated that west of the north–south line from Derry to Waterford, Irish was still the first language. The hedge schools, with their strongly classical and Gaelic bent, which were originally meant to counter the penal debarment of Catholics from education and provide the necessary preliminary training for clerical students, continued to exist alongside the parish schools that were permitted by mid-century. Irish poetry continued to be written, its early formality gradually being mitigated as it became the voice of the peasant majority. Such poets as Aogán Ó Rathaile, (1670–1726), Cathal Buí Mac Giolla Gunna (?1680–1755), Seán Clárach Mac Dónaill (1691–1754), Peadar Ó Doirnín (1704–69), Art Mac Cumhaidh (1738–73), Eoghan Rua Ó Súilleabháin (1748–84), Brian Merriman (1749–1803) and many others mourned the loss of greatness and commented upon the condition of the Irish in modes that varied from a satire worthy of the old bards to a modern bawdry. Anonymous songs telling of love, piety and a remarkable zest for life continued to be composed and sung into the middle of the nineteenth century.

Dance, music of harp and pipe, and later of whistle and fiddle, survived all the social deprivation and attempts at obliteration. Some of the parvenu landlords encouraged such itinerant harpists and composers as the great Turlough Carolan (1670–1738) to entertain their guests, reviving a staple feature of Gaelic feasts. The tradition was sufficiently strong throughout the century to permit the organisation of a four-day harp festival in Belfast in 1796 and allow the musical scribe Edward Bunting (1773–1843) to publish three collections of 'ancient' Irish music. The traditional art of storytelling, containing lore more than a thousand years old (the word *fiannaíocht* indicating its ancient origins) was preserved by *seanchaithe* and supplied a subtle *béaloideas* that survived even the linguistic *seppuku* that followed the cataclysmic 1840s. The peasantry that appeared debased to their Ascendancy masters and to British overlords had a real if 'hidden' culture. Their 'fecklessness' (a function of their social condition) was no more characteristic of the nation than their 'stupidity', as measured by their mangled English.

As ever, Ulster was different from the rest of the country. It had not only the greatest concentration of Protestants but also of dissenters (more than 90 per cent of all Protestants). The appearance of the province, except in the poorer parts of Donegal, the Sperrins, the Mournes and boggy areas of west Tyrone, Fermanagh, Monaghan and Cavan was decidedly neater than that of Munster or Connacht, and manifestly next to Godliness. An early twentieth-century comment by Catholics, that a room, when tidied, was 'more Protestant looking', was a sincere compliment to their orderly neighbours and set a standard for a growing Catholic bourgeoisie in the northern province. The houses had windows and chimneys and the towns were well lit and orderly; some had civic water supplies. The Protestants had come out from their fortified 'bawns' (bábhún='enclosure') and were living more or less at peace with their Catholic neighbours. Memories of 1641 were easily rekindled but there were exceptions to the generalisation that described the mid-century 'city' of Armagh: Anglicans filled the professions; Catholics, as ever living peripherally, were the labourers, and Presbyterians were the artificers and men of business.

Strafford, as a mitigation of his resolute imposition of the 'Black Oath' on Presbyterian males, encouraged the linen trade and William III showed his special indulgence to Ulster by appointing the Huguenot Samuel-Louis Crommelin 'Overseer of the Royal Linen Manufacture of Ireland'. His arrival in Lisburn in 1698 brought mechanisation to what had been a cottage industry, and the bleach green became an identifiable feature of Ulster villages, especially in Antrim, Down, Armagh and Monaghan. Even in this respect generalisations are just that, for there was a sizeable number of Catholics employed at different stages of the process from flax-growing to export of lawn. Newry, Armagh, Derry and Belfast were essentially Protestant centres but recurring crop failure, population increase and minimal tolerance attracted Catholic migrations. In Derry the Catholics of Inishowen established themselves in a shanty town which grew and eventually showed improvement in the reclaimed boggy land beneath the city's western wall. Since larger towns are microcosms of countries, these significant boroughs were to be the scene of sporadic if generally low-key sectarian violence as the condition and power of Catholics improved. Nineteenth-century Belfast garnered a large minority of Catholics of originally rural origin who were concentrated in its city-centre slums and the land to the west between the port and the hills of Divis and the Black Mountain. It was here that sectarian conflict was naturally greatest, acting as a kind of register of political activity and socio-industrial conditions, and reaching a startling intensity as agitation for Home Rule increased in the last quarter of the nineteenth century.

One generalisation that had almost total truth was that the best land (usually that in the basins of the main rivers, Lagan, Bann, Foyle and Blackwater) in south Antrim, north Derry, east Donegal and east Tyrone, north Armagh and most of County Down (except the mountainous southeast) was held by Protestants. Presbyterians were in a majority but their holdings were small and they suffered some disabilities because of their dissent. They had full religious freedom from 1719 but were prevented from public life, even involvement in borough politics, until 1780. The tests of the 1704 Act were not implemented with absolute rigour against even these Protestants; there were some Presbyterian members of parliament, and in their Down and Antrim towns their church councils were the real civic authority. Yet they were formally excluded from power and this sense of less than full citizenship led to a suspicion of the gentry and their Anglican Church, and a growing anti-establishment agitation which had its flowering in the formation of the revolutionary United Irishmen in the last decade of the eighteenth century.

It also meant that further emigration held no terrors for descendants of Ulster settlers. The tradition of being 'planted by a river', which they had preserved as a metaphysical icon for a century, meant that the river could as well be the Hudson, the Delaware or even the Mississippi. The port of Derry became the main emigration point for regular exoduses of Ulstermen (about a quarter of a million between 1720 and 1775), who were to play a significant part in the severing of the American colonies from Britain. The calm of the eighty years after Limerick was to be broken by this American Revolution and its reverberations. Irish soldiers had had a remote involvement in Marlborough's Spanish Succession campaigns (on both sides) and Ireland helped to bear the costs of later eighteenth-century wars, notably that of the Austrian Succession (1740–8) and the Seven Years' War (1756–63) with France which inevitably led to the loss of America. The dashing French privateer Thurot had taken and held Carrickfergus for a week in 1760. (He afterwards raided the Isle of Man and perished in an engagement with three British frigates in Lough Foyle.)

The new threat from America seemed to many, including George III, who had become king in 1760, the start of the dissolution of the empire. It was to have a profound effect on Irish politics. It was realised that the country was more or less undefended, since the British army was needed elsewhere. There had been a considerable military presence in the country from the beginning of the century but the minimal Irish reaction to the 'Forty-five' and the need to have armies to fight the foreign wars decreased the establishment. At first there was considerable support for the colonists, especially in Ulster – 'kith and kin'. An amelioration of the condition of Catholics in Canada and the notably Protestant attitudes of the declarers of independence respectively frightened and reassured both the Ascendancy and the Dissenters. The entry of France on the side of the Americans in 1778 renewed old fears of a back door 'Catholic' invasion. The Ascendancy grandees and their tenants burgeoned into local militias which were known as Volunteers. The long sleep of 'slavery' was over: the Anglo-Irish were about to show their 'patriotism' and their power. There were many colourful rallies in Dublin, Belfast and Armagh in 1781 as a preparation for a convention in Dungannon on 15 February 1782. This was attended by 242 delegates from 148 corps and a form of independent legislative assembly was demanded. The fall of Lord North's government (the one that 'lost' America) hastened the repeal of the 'Sixth of George I' and a sufficient amendment of Poynings' Law to grant the Dublin parliament the right to legislate for an independent Ireland owing a separate allegiance to George III.

The 1770s also saw the first formal repeals of the Penal

Laws. In 1772 Catholics were enabled to lease bogland and in 1778 leasing and inheritance disabilities were removed. Relief acts in 1782, 1792 and 1793 removed all the remaining impediments to full citizenship except for 'emancipation' which was taken to mean the right to sit as a member of parliament (and by the time it was obtained, in 1829, meant being an MP at Westminster) and hold high office. As ever the members of the Irish parliament (with notable exceptions like Grattan and Luke Gardiner), now in its palatial residence at College Green, opposed these 'relief' acts to the last. It was only after Castle insistence that the cumbersome and, except in the important area of land leasing and inheritance, largely unenforceable battery of measures was finally repealed.

The repeal of the Penal Laws in Britain in 1778 had resulted eventually in five days of frightening and dangerous rioting (described so dramatically in Dickens's *Barnaby Rudge*) in London in June 1780. The trouble was stirred on by Lord George Gordon and his 50,000 stalwarts of the Protestant Association. Some of the violence was directed against Irish labourers who, workless at home, had come looking for employment from the end of the 1760s. They had established a survival colony in the poorest slums of London's east end and, unfastidious about the work they would undertake, were believed incorrectly to accept lower wages than the English workers. There was no single equivalent response in Ireland but the relief acts were undoubtedly the prime cause of the Catholic–Protestant violence in the 1790s. The gradual amelioration of the Catholic situation with the series of relief acts was upsetting to the two kinds of Ulster Protestants for slightly different reasons. The Anglicans generally resented the increasing social acceptance of the despised underclass, this especially true of many of the landlords; the Presbyterian resentment had its basis as much in the perceived economic consequences of the liberalisation.

The Westminster policy, though couched in liberal language, was seen by its detractors as the age-old device of 'divide and conquer,' and certainly the war with revolutionary France, begun in 1793, concentrated Pitt's mind wonderfully. He required a quiescent Ireland at home and he needed the 'other-ranks' soldiers which the relief acts would inevitably supply. Unlike England, where the Catholics were a tiny and largely urban minority, Ireland had about four million Catholics, and by no means all of them were impoverished and uneducated. And from 25 July 1792 they had in Wolfe Tone a new and dynamic spokesman for their Association. Henry Flood, unquestionably the finest orator in the new parliament, had declared soon after its inception that the penal laws were 'not laws of persecution; they were a political necessity'. He spoke for a majority of the members, but already it was too late to halt the slow process of Catholic resurgence. The last decade of the Protestant century was to be radically different from the rest; and Ascendancy independence had but a few years of life before it was dissolved.

9

The Boys of Wexford

The histories of Britain and Ireland were never so intricately – if untenderly – entwined as in the 1790s. The main pressure on Pitt's government was the war with revolutionary France, but the heady ideas of '*liberté, égalité* and *fraternité*' had crossed the channel and exhilarated the British poor, both rustic and urban, in the same measure that they terrified squire and parson. Workers 'combinations', embryo trades unions, generated by the changes in working conditions associated with the agrarian and industrial revolutions, were regarded as doorstep republicanism and banned by Combination Acts in 1799. The condition of Ireland and the violence of the Wexford and Carlow *jacqueries* the previous year gave Pitt the excuse to acquire the kinds of powers for the British government that had been assumed by Dublin Castle during at least the previous decade.

The association known as the United Irishmen had been founded in Belfast on 14 October 1791 by a group of young radicals, Henry Joy McCracken, Samuel Neilson, William Drennan and others who were fired with ideas of reform. They were lawyers, merchants, journalists and were as blissful as Wordsworth at the fall of the Bastille. They were joined by the Kildare-born radical, Wolfe Tone (1763–98). The limited nature of the Relief Act of 1793 bitterly disappointed the young republican, now strongly imbued with Jacobin ideas. (His support of Catholics was entirely political; born a Protestant, he knew that all religion was superstition and would blow away like wood ash in the rational wind of revolution.) The dismissal of the liberal Earl Fitzwilliam as Lord Lieutenant in February 1795 after two months of turbulent and clumsy attempts at reform was seen as further proof of Pitt's entrenchment. The country seemed to be aflame with radical ideas and grim with the need to keep them in check. The various branches of the United Irishmen (a Dublin society had been formed a month after the Belfast one, led by Napper Tandy and Hamilton Rowan) continued to debate the condition of the country and to call for reform. The society had few Catholic members and not many Anglicans joined; and it generated a reactive yeomanry militia, led by affronted Volunteer captains, mainly Anglican landlords, whose earlier calls for parliamentary reform had not included any relief for Catholics.

The Dublin branch of the United Irishmen was suppressed on 23 May 1794 and as an underground and secret society it attracted a larger and more ruthless membership with the kind of *sans-culottes* element that had been the terror of the Terror. Tone, in exile in France after a judicious move to America to avoid guilt by association with a known French agent, managed to persuade Carnot, the leading member of the revolutionary governing committee, to give him a general in Lazare Hoche and an army of 15,000 men. They sailed for Bantry Bay in forty-three ships in December 1796. The expedition failed because of winter storms and the ships were forced to return home. The Bantry venture was and remains another of the great 'if onlys' or 'what ifs' of Irish history. The United Irishmen still flourished in Ulster, and March 1797 saw the start of a campaign by General Lake (on the specific instructions of Pelham, the Chief Secretary) to root out radicalism. His powers were absolute and his methods of an extreme ruthlessness. Fire, torture, hanging carried out by an enthusiastic yeomanry convinced many that they were not really radicals, but made those members that had not been interned willing to risk a rising if only in desperation.

The authorities, in fact, were kept well informed of cell decisions since their intelligence system was highly efficient. Government swoops in Leinster in May 1798 badly weakened the society there and the week of 23–30 May saw unsuccessful actions in Naas, Clane, Lucan, Tallaght, Lusk, Rathfarnham, Monasterevin, Kilkenny, Slane, Baltinglass and Tara. The informers had done their business well. The story in Wexford was different. There was there a great deal of Protestant–Catholic bitterness and a sufficient body of Catholic farmers and artisans, not badly armed and with a competent leader in Bagenal Harvey (1762–98). At first the insurgents, with help from contingents from Waterford and Carlow, met with some success, and Harvey was able to control his ragged followers with threats of death for all guilty of 'excesses'. He was relieved of his post after failing to capture New Ross on 5 June. The last engagement was at Vinegar Hill in Enniscorthy, when Lake's forces overwhelmed the 'rebels' on 21 June.

Hearing of the risings in the southeast, on 7 June McCracken led a party to attack Antrim, but after some initial success was defeated by Colonel Durham's militia. He fled across the moors to Colin Glen to the west of Belfast town and hid out on Cave Hill where he, Neilson, Thomas Russell and Tone had renewed the United Irishmen's oath in May 1795. He might very well have managed to get on board a ship bound for America, a passage that his sister had arranged, had not he been accidentally discovered and captured by the Carrickfergus militia. He was hanged in the Cornmarket in Belfast on 17 July. The other show of defiance was at Ballynahinch, when Henry Monro held out against General Nugent's army for three days (11–13 June) before being hanged in front of his own house in Lisburn on 15 June. By the end of the month the "98 rising', as it was later called, was virtually over. Harvey had been hanged on Wexford Bridge on 26 June and resprisals were in progress. Lake ignored the terms of Cornwallis's amnesty and the total death toll, often because of naked sectarianism, was finally computed at 30,000.

There were a few dramatic sideshows, one tragic, another farcical. Tone, assiduous as ever in France, managed to gather French forces for a landing at Killala under General Humbert on 22 August. The French set up the Republic of Connacht and defeated the government forces at the famous 'Races of Castlebar' five days later. On 8 September, after a fortnight of ragged skirmishing, Humbert surrendered to Lake and Cornwallis at Ballinamuck, County Longford, and his Irish followers, mostly Mayo peasants who had never been United Irishmen, were slaughtered. A small force accompanied by the egregious Napper Tandy landed at Rutland Island opposite Burtonport in west Donegal on 16 September, but hearing of Humbert's surrender Tandy got blind drunk and was carried back to his ship. He eventually escaped with his life, largely through the insistence of Napoleon. Finally Tone, found in the company of yet another French force, under Bompard, was arrested by the British navy on 20 September, tried and condemned to death. He committed suicide in his cell by slitting his throat and died a week later on 19 November.

The summer and autumn of 1798 had seen the greatest shedding of blood in Ireland's history, much of it in Wexford and nearly all of it sectarian. The rising there was more in the nature of a peasant's revolt for bread-and-butter issues, such as taxes, land and religious hatred. There was little of the Jacobin about it, although some of the insurgents, the 'Croppies', cut their hair short in fraternity with the revolutionaries in France. The second half of the century had been marked by the formation of localised, mainly rural, secret societies generated by agricultural discontent. Of these the 'Whiteboys', often an umbrella term, were the best known. They represented a Catholic sense of injustice but not necessarily a sectarian stance. There were northern Presbyterian equivalents in 'Oakboys' of the 1760s and the 'Steelboys' of the 1770s. The methods and the targets were similar; they fought increased rents and rates, and enclosures, and used firing of property, maiming of animals and the occasional murder of a landlord's agent to make their point.

As the condition of Catholics slowly improved there was an inevitable reaction from northern Protestants and a growing sectarianism in the attitudes of the various 'Boys'. The more militant Catholic groups became known as 'Defenders' and there was evidence of oath-taking, 'conscription' and isolated raids, especially in the Cavan–Monaghan area from 1792. This spread into Armagh and Catholic activity was matched by rival groups among Protestants, notably the 'Peep O'Day Boys', largely linen workers whose economic stability was perceived as depending upon alliances with landlords. Demographically they should have been attracted to the United Irishmen but their strong Anglicanism, associated with the primatial see of Armagh, made them ideal members of the yeomanry. Their local knowledge was of prime use to Lake in his suppression of the radical society. Lake's policy, of course, was deliberately inflammatory and the yeomen with their gentry captains collaborated enthusiastically before, during and after the rising.

Defenderism was as much a product as a cause of Protestant violence, which began in the mid-1780s and reached dangerous levels in the middle years of the 1790s. The confrontation that has acquired the greatest notoriety was the battle of the 'Diamond', the crossroads near Loughgall, County Armagh where on 21 September 1795 the local chapter of the 'Peep O'Day Boys', well-supplied with Volunteer arms, met and killed thirty of a band of Catholic Defenders, many of whom were urban linen workers and driven from their jobs by unemployed Protestants. The Peep O'Day line was that they were merely applying the necessary Penal Laws that the authorities had weakly abandoned. The sequel was more significant than the actual 'battle'. The first lodge of the Orange Order was founded that evening in Loughgall in the home of James Sloan to which the victorious Protestant contingent had repaired after the 'battle'. The basic principle of the order was stated as a defence 'of the King and his heirs so long as he or they support the Protestant ascendancy' – a classical statement of the continuing conditional loyalty of Ulster Protestants. The order survived many bannings, its reinstatement often as the result of noble insistence, and was to play a significant part in Ulster politics and sectarian violence thereafter. The following 12 July, the new calendar anniversary of the battle of the Boyne, was marked by demonstrations of the ninety Orange lodges that had been founded in the ten months since the 'Diamond'. The titular and persistent tribute to William III is ironic in light of his known non-sectarian views. In addition, the particular viciousness of some of the events of 1798 in the south-east may be understood by the fact that it was a region where there was a religious tension of Ulster levels. The situation was exacerbated by the arrival of two notably partisan companies of yeomanry, those of Donegal and North Cork, in early May.

The events of the year 1798 were to form a significant part of the mythology that replaced historiography in the nationalist imagination from the 1840s on. The bravery of the insurgents was undeniable and the memory of sectarian excesses was muted by the bloody savagery of the reprisals. The non-denominational optimism of Young Ireland and the rhetorical tone of the articles and poetry of the *Nation* found in the 1798 heroes, north and south, grist to their milling. Contemporary ballads recorded the deeds of such heroes as 'Billy Byrne of Ballymanus' who was hanged on 25 July 1798, betrayed by a noted informer Thomas Reynolds, and later days recorded deeds as brave when Croppy Boys sang 'Old Ireland Free' and balladeers followed Henry Joy. The full sanctification of 'Ninety-Eight' was achieved at the first centenary celebrations, by which time the songs of P. J. McCall and R. D. Joyce canonising Kelly of Killane, Father Murphy 'from old Kilcormack' and the 'Boys of Wexford' were current, and Willie Yeats was being taught Irish history at Maud Gonne's feet. One odd composition was 'The Memory of the Dead', written anonymously for the *Nation* in 1843 by the Protestant academic John Kells Ingram and representing his sole nationalist statement. One line, 'They rose in dark and evil days', sums up the romantic appeal of the rising for both the constitutional and the alternative nationalist. After a century of quiescence at injustice, a psychological dam had burst. Grattan's poignant address to the Ireland of the shotgun marriage of the Union, 'I see her in a swoon, but she is not dead', was truer than he realised. The dispossessed were at last on the move; Yeats's intermittently rough beast had begun its slouch towards Bethlehem.

What is interesting is that the Orangemen had their own ballads, mirror-images of the nationalist repertoire. Such songs as 'Croppies, Lie Down!', 'Dolly's Brae', and (that most traduced of flowers, *lilium bulbiferum*) 'The Orange Lily-O' were to be heard sung with equal fervour – and venom – on equivalent occasions. Defenderism lived on – Dr Jekyll needs Mr Hyde – to have several avatars, to generate the Smith O'Brien rising of 1848 and to form the basis of Fenianism and its progeny: the various armies and brotherhoods whose careers emphasise a belief (rarely held by a majority) that Britain will never respond to anything but the 'armed struggle'. It is a device or debate that has characterised Irish life right until the present day and is bound of its nature to be a self-fulfilling prophecy.

'Ninety-eight' also demonstrated that the lumpen Irish had new and unexpected leaders: sixty priests were killed or executed in Wexford. Catholic relief had increased the standing and the social position of the clergy. Though the hierarchy remained officially opposed to any form of Defenderism, and within a week of the outbreak of trouble in Wexford the president of the new seminary in Maynooth (founded in 1796) and twenty-three bishops had condemned the rising, the rank and file were close enough to their flocks to be much more aware of their real feelings and ambitions. Daniel O'Connell, the great early nineteenth-century leader of Catholic Ireland (arguably for all his warts its greatest leader ever) understood the status that priests held in their communities and used it in his, on the whole, altruistic campaigns.

Pitt could now say that his worst nightmare had materialised. Ireland was a 'ship on fire' but his remedy was extinguishment rather than cutting adrift. The turbulent end to the century was probably inevitable but the British government cannot be exculpated from complicity in its fomentation. Certainly it made Pitt's task of selling an act of union that he saw as the only cure for the distressful country and its muddied people much easier. His relief acts of 1795 had not offered full emancipation; it was the trump card he kept to win Catholic support for union. In fact there was on the whole little opposition from the mass of Catholics. The Orangemen were opposed to union because they feared enfranchised papists, and the Ascendancy gentry were reluctant to lose their recently won independence. Castlereagh and Cornwallis were given the task of easing the bill through the Irish parliament, which they did with fastidious distaste, handling 'the most corrupt people under heaven'. Many millions of pounds by today's values were used in bribery and honours granted so readily that the offices were devalued. The bill was passed by 158 votes to 115, only seven of the Ayes unbribed in Grattan's reckoning, and the Act of Union became law on 1 January 1801. Catholic emancipation was not granted. Westminster opposition was supported by Farmer George who found it against his coronation oath and produced one of the least convincing reactions of a man not noted for temperance of tongue: 'I would rather give up my throne and beg my bread from door to door throughout Europe than consent to such a measure.' Pitt, coldly honourable as ever, resigned, but was persuaded to return to power in 1804 as the only man who could save Europe from Bonaparte.

There is a well-known anecdote of the period concerning one of the strongest voices against union, John Philpot Curran. Shortly after the act became law, he was passing the splendid buildings which once housed the parliament in College Green with a newly created Irish peer who said he hated the sight of the place. 'I never yet heard of a murderer who was not afraid of the ghost of his victim!' cried Curran. There was a real sense of departed glory and Edward Lysaght, the Dublin wit (1763–1810), was only exaggerating slightly when he forecast in his pasquinade 'A Prospect':

> Thro' Capel-street soon as you'll rurally range,
> You'll scarce recognise it the same street;
> Choice turnips shall grow in your Royal
>   Exchange,
> And fine cabbages down along Dame-street.

Curran had an oblique part to play in a coda to the turbulence of the 1790s. His daughter Sarah was secretly engaged to Robert Emmet (1778–1803), the younger brother of Thomas Addis Emmet, who was the leading counsel for the United Irishmen. (Exiled in 1799, he tried to interest Napoleon in another invasion of Ireland in 1802 but the First Consul was too busy concluding the short-lived Peace of Amiens and, after hostilities resumed, concentrated his mind upon a direct invasion of England.) Robert was a leader of the United Irishmen at Trinity College, where he was a friend of the Minstrel Boy, Tom Moore, but failed to enrol him as a member. In the mood that Yeats later characterised as the 'delirium of the brave' he led a crowd of Dublin 'Liberty Rangers' to attack Dublin Castle on 23 July 1803. Lord Kilwarden, the liberal chief justice, and his son-in-law were dragged from their coach and murdered. There was a skirmish in the Coombe but the event quickly petered out and Emmet fled to hiding in the mountains. Arrested on 25 August by Major Sirr, at the house in the village of Harold's Cross where he had a tryst with Sarah Curran, he was defended eloquently by Leonard McNally, the author of 'Sweet Lass of Richmond Hill' and the government's chief spy during the whole of the United Irishmen episode. He was hanged in Thomas Street on 20 September and decapitated the following day. His 'epitaph' speech from the dock and the romantic trappings of his adventure made him the 'darling of Erin' for nearly two hundred years. His friend Tommy Moore immortalised the lovers in two of his Irish Melodies, 'She Is Far from the Land' and 'O, Breathe Not His Name!' with which he later delighted liberal audiences in Holland House.

10

King of the Beggars

Union seemed to bring little change: Catholics had not achieved emancipation and the richer members of the Protestant Ascendancy were still privileged and recipients of nearly as much patronage as before. Though communications had been improved in the north and east there was an inevitable lack of centralisation of law enforcement. Local magistrates (and police forces) were partial, and unduly deferential to local grandees, and the areas they governed were usually self-contained, dividing the country into a large number of small and virtually independent oligarchies. The agitation for Catholic emancipation, however remote the prospect, revived old Protestant paranoia, especially in Ulster, which was to grow psychologically more remote as the century progressed. Presbyterianism had to overcome the trauma of its liberal wing's support of the United Irishmen and the 1820s were marked by what seemed to be a doctrinal struggle but which was really a political clash between the coevals, Henry Cooke and Henry Montgomery (1788–1865). Cooke was in his popular appeal and political power the Protestant Daniel O'Connell, even to the extent of holding 'monster' meetings, and he was the successful marriage counsellor who reconciled Presbyterian and Ulster Anglican, at least socially and politically, and persuaded a majority of northern Protestants to accept the Union. He vanquished Montgomery, who was a radical in belief and an emancipationist in politics, quickly routing the latter's 'remonstrant synod', and with his establishment of the General Assembly of the Presbyterian Church set up a formidable institution which could very well have been described as 'Ulster intransigence at prayer'. Montgomery's followers were afterwards known as 'non-subscribing' and they manfully maintained their reputation for liberalism, numbering among their twentieth-century divines Albert McElroy (1915–75) who was a founder member of the Ulster Liberal Association in 1956.

The economically buoyant years of the wars with France ended with what could reasonably be described as Irish agriculture's Waterloo. Visitors to Ireland, attracted by what they heard of its 'variety', were startled and appalled by the extremity of rural poverty that they discovered in the west and southwest of the variegated country, finding the almost naked filthy denizens of the windowless, chimneyless, furnitureless cabins 'on the extreme edge of human misery' – as a shocked and recently knighted Sir Walter Scott noted in his diary in 1825. These lower depths represented the base level of Irish society, people earning nothing by their casual and itinerant work except doubtful tenure of a plot of worthless ground on which to grow potatoes and build a hut of sods. These plots, many of less than an acre, were the final terms in a geometrical progression of subdivision of land that literally could not be subdivided further, unlike Swift's progression of fleas with fleas ('And these have smaller yet to bite 'em/And so proceed *ad infinitum*'). He used the model to describe how poets are preyed upon by hacks but the idea could well have come from the practice of subdivision which was well-established by the time of his deanery.

What made the prospect more shocking to the Hibernophile visitors who all had heard Tom Moore's Melodies and may well have had harps, round towers or Irish wolfhounds engraved on their snuff-boxes was the huge numbers of people who lived in each other's shadows, and the contrast with the residences of the strong farmers and the Big Houses which were in the current pun quite 'contagious'. The census of 1841 revealed a population of 8,175,124, an increase of six million in the century and a half since Limerick. About half the land was held by Catholics on long lease and one-fifth was owned outright. This meant that a significant number of the hated landlords were now Catholic. Furthermore, most of the 'terms' in the sequence of subdividers, confusingly called 'middlemen', were Catholics as well.

The general, but not inclusive, execration of the landowners was justified. Many of the grander eighteenth-century 'absentees' had sold their properties to lesser men with money and by the 1820s a large proportion of the land was held by 'presentees' whose lifestyles, set unconsciously by their English opposite numbers, meant that many lived permanently beyond their means. The main purpose of their investment was to provide them with the maximum income and they had little concern about how that income was obtained. The land of Ireland, except in the east, is more suited to grazing than tillage but the boom war years dictated the product. Tillage is labour-intensive and one of the causes of the population congestion on many properties was the continuously high price of grain during the long wars with France. By the time of the beginning of O'Connell's emancipationist crusade the slump in the price of grain had shown little sign of abatement and a significant number of landlords was turning again to cattle, causing great destitution. With few exceptions, there was little attempt at improvement, especially by the use of those techniques that had proved so successful in the agricultural revolution in England. If any tenant farmer tried to improve his holding he ran the strong risk of having his rent increased. Since the rent was already racked to its utmost economic extent there was little incentive for any changes in practice. Outside of Ulster, too, the tenant would have been 'at-will', without security of tenure.

The new leader, Daniel O'Connell (1775–1847), had been educated in France and had seen the tumbrils and the bloodshed of the early part of the revolution. It made him a constitutionalist thereafter. The barbarities of 1798 merely confirmed him in his conviction, stated rather theatrically in a speech made in 1843:

> Not for all the universe contains would I, in
> the struggle for what I conceive my country's
> cause, consent to the effusion of a single drop
> of human blood, except my own.

He had been brought up in Kerry, where his family on both sides had managed to keep the trappings and some of the wealth of an old Gaelic family. Their land had been preserved by a friendly Protestant holding it in his own name. With the coming of the 1792 Relief Act O'Connell had become a lawyer and made a name for himself for a forensic brilliance having all the rhetorical virtues except *gravitas*. He became in Frank O'Connor's phrase the 'king of the beggars' and gave hope to the poorer Catholics while basing his strength on a Catholic middle class which had now consolidated its position.

The proliferation of rural protest societies continued: 'Whiteboys' whose names might vary from place to place: Caravats, Shanavests and Ribbonmen, the last a more specifically political and, where appropriate, anti-Protestant grouping than the others, whose concerns were that of their eighteenth-century equivalents. Hedge and other school-masters were assumed to provide the education of subversion. One of a number of these societies is the subject of a story in *To-day in Ireland*, published anonymously in 1827 by Eyre Evans Crowe, which gives the best picture of the Ireland of the time. The longest story in the three-volume work, 'The Carders' [a name actually in use] describes just such a secret society, the title taken from their use on their foes of the ferociously spiked comb used for untangling sheep's wool. There the 'captain' turns out to be the kindly local teacher who is hanged. The story has also a rabidly anti-Catholic Anglican curate, a reminder of the continuing despisal of churchmen for the main source of their incomes. (Another story, 'Connemara', is a humorous tale about the essentially free life led by Catholic tribal leaders in the minimally policed land beyond the Shannon, painting a picture of a homestead not unlike that of O'Connell, though without the private chapel that was the pride of Derrynane House.)

The main source of discontent among Catholics, and shared with the Presbyterians, was the tithes which all who lived in the Anglican parish had to pay towards the support of the local clergyman. This glaringly unfair imposition gave rise to confrontations so serious in 1831 that the agitation was known as the Tithe War. On 14 December, sixteen policemen were killed at Carrickshock, County Kilkenny after a confrontation with a crowd of 2,000. The 'war' lasted until 1834, the last serious incident, at Gortroe in County Cork, resulting in eight deaths. The existence of the gangs was evidence of a felt if not articulated sense of grievance. Their concentration on the Church tax and such rural matters as enclosures and clearances showed a clearer perception of what was most urgently in need of amelioration. Earning a living from the land was the problem that beset a majority of those who formed O'Connell's constitutional army. Emancipation was an emotional, even an academic, topic; to paraphrase a future proverb: they got their emancipation and still broke stones. (The violence of the encounters was aggravated by overreaction by police and clergy and shortly afterwards police organisation was centralised, the force made professional, disciplined and less partisan, and a separate constabulary was established for Dublin; known as the DMP (Dublin Metropolitan Police), this ever after took pride in being a civic unarmed urban force.)

The Tithe Act of 1836 settled the matter by arranging that tithed income should be converted to a rent charge which would create a fund for clerical costs. The act was devised by Thomas Drummond, who was under-secretary for Ireland from 1835 until his death in 1840. It was he who famously chided the Ascendancy that 'property had its duties as well as its rights' and threatened Orange magistrates who permitted their brethren to violate the law that their commissions should be rescinded. The five-year alliance between O'Connell and Drummond later seemed a kind of golden age. For once there was an English politician (in fact he was born and educated in Edinburgh) who seemed to understand the true causes of Irish discontent.

O'Connell's career and contribution are better appreciated by historians than by his contemporary adversaries like John Mitchel (1815–75) and Thomas Meagher (1823–67) and later traducers who followed a more activist line. His Catholic Association, founded in 1823, was wider in membership than its eighteenth-century namesake. It used as agents the Catholic clergy who, Maynooth and Carlow educated, had access to the whole population. The great mass of the poor and lowly, who had played no part in constitutional agitation, were encouraged to become members, and the 'Catholic rent' of one penny a month was within the means of all but the destitute and provided the association with very adequate funds. Control was not absolute or the Tithe War should never have taken place, but membership of the association gave many thousands, whose existence up till then had been characterised by *anomie,* a palpable stake in the country. The local strategy meetings, especially at times of elections, were practical lessons in politics, a form of adult education at which the Irish proved apt pupils. The techniques of ward-heeling that were to be so effective from 1850 on in Boston and New York were learned under the auspices of the association.

In the days before the 1872 Ballot Act it took courage for a tenant farmer to vote against the instructions of his landlord. Irish Catholic voters found that they regularly had to vote for known opponents of emancipation but now with the discipline and protection of association membership and the presence of local priests they trusted themselves to vote in groups. In the 1826 general election anti-emancipationists were defeated by association-sponsored candidates (still Protestant) in the constituencies of Waterford, Westmeath, Louth and Monaghan. And it was clear that in the next election, except in the usual Protestant strongholds, of course, the organised Catholic vote could unseat many of the sitting members. Emancipation was won before that, however, in the famous Clare election of 1828. Vesey-Fitzgerald, the member, was given a cabinet appointment and in accordance with current custom was required to fight his seat again. The association at once looked for a friendly Protestant to stand against Fitzgerald but none suitable was found. Then it was pointed out that while the law prevented a Catholic from sitting in parliament it said nothing about one standing. O'Connell announced his candidature and the now highly efficient machinery went to work. After five days of polling the result was declared in Ennis on 5 July: O'Connell: 2057; Vesey-Fitzgerald: 982.

In August, Wellington had to advise George IV that the Home Secretary, Sir Robert Peel, could not be responsible for public order. What was being faced was the possibility of a rival parliament of elected Catholic MPs. The excitement among rank-and-file members of the association was great and there was a real possibility that O'Connell might not be able to control them. By now, too, there were considerable numbers of Catholics in the police and army whose loyalty in extremity might be dubious. By 13 April 1829 there was a majority in the Commons and Wellington had persuaded enough peers in the Lords to carry an 'Act for the relief of His Majesty's Roman Catholic subjects.' The concomitant mean-spiritedness of the Tory administration was seen in O'Connell being refused admission to the House on 15 May because the measure 'is not retrospective' (he was returned unopposed on 30 July) and in that with the abolition of the 'forty-shilling freeholder' franchise the Irish electorate was reduced by 80 per cent. It was not until 1850 and the Representation of the People (Ireland) Act that emancipation began to be felt, and by then Ireland was a vastly changed country.

Still it was a mighty victory and with all offices of state except the very highest open to Catholics, the penal disabilities were virtually at an end. Now O'Connell had another crusade: the repeal of the Act of Union. A Repeal Association was founded in 1840 and run on the same lines as his Catholic Association, garnering much larger sums in a repeal rent. The most visible tactic employed was the 'monster' meeting, usually when the Tories were in power; when his Whig allies formed the government O'Connell's tactics were more low-key and devised to cause minimum embarrassment. This meant a decade of apparent inaction, though many significant reforms were achieved, especially under the consulate of Drummond. The term 'monster' meeting was coined by *The Times* then at its most thunderous. (Thomas Barnes (1785–1841), its shaping radical editor, had vowed that it should constantly 'thunder for reform'.) It was not popular with conservatives: Trollope referred to it in his novels pejoratively as the *Jupiter* (from one of the Roman sobriquets for their chief god: *Iuppiter Tonans*) and it especially attacked O'Connell. There was no Press Council in Victorian England and personal vituperation was indulged in a manner unthinkable today even in the most rancid tabloid. In a *Times* editorial priests were called 'surpliced ruffians' and the Emancipationist was pen-pictured by a squib which began:

> Scum condensed of Irish bog,
> Ruffian coward demagogue,
> Boundless liar, base detractor
> Nurse of murders, treason's factor . . .

O'Connell was also a graphic target for the recently established *Punch*, which in these early cheeky years reserved its most graphic attacks for Ireland and the Roman Catholic

Church, then regaining strength in England, especially after emancipation which, of course, annealed English Catholics as well. It is notable that, however radical and reformist the British press may have been at home, it was generally (there were exceptions) xenophobic (and hibernophobic) when it looked beyond its island fastness. The colonial instinct was never stronger than in these years and the prevailing attitude was expressed simply but effectively in a twentieth-century sentimental ballad, 'Galway Bay':

> For the English came and tried to teach us
>   their way;
> They blamed us just for being what we are...

The purpose of O'Connell's huge rallies was involvement of the newly politicised, if disenfranchised, mass of the poorer Irish. By this means the energy that was diffused earlier in faction fights and '-boy' activities was channelled into peaceful, if heady protest. The year 1843 saw protests all over Connacht, Leinster and Munster and the building of O'Connell's headquarters, significantly named Conciliation Hall. The attendance numbers are only estimates but they are impressive: 19 April, Limerick, 120,000; 23 April, Kells, 150,000; 18 May, Charleville, 300,000; 21 May, Cork, 500,000, Cashel, 300,000; 25 May, Nenagh, 400,000. The most memorable was at Tara on 15 August, the place chosen, like Cashel, because of its historical resonance and the date the great 'autumn feast of Mary'. It was attended by at least 750,000; *The Times* said 'a million'. And O'Connell made a superlative comeback.

The tactic of the hosting was approved if not actually suggested by O'Connell's young Turks, the band of journalists and 'varsity' men founded by Thomas Davis (1814–45), Charles Gavan Duffy (1816–1903) and John Blake Dillon (1816–66), who called themselves Young Ireland. The founding trio had in the *Nation*, by means of rhetorical essays and rousing ballad poetry, re-established a sense of nationality and patriotism which fitted well with the Catholic and Repeal Associations' training in politics and doctrine as offered by local priests and teachers. Its non-denominational stance and Trinity background reassured Protestant liberals, who contributed to the pages of the widely read journal, even if these aspects did not please a Catholic hierarchy already strong enough to fight against the National schools and the Queen's colleges.

Some of the ballads, especially those written by Davis himself, were seen by some as clarions. Certainly the more hot-headed members, like Mitchel and Meagher, regarded them as such and in time affected to find the *Nation* too passive and the founders too O'Connellite – a view which must have surprised the Liberator. Davis died of scarlet fever in 1845 just as the first reports of *phytophthora infestans* were being received and there remains a question mark over his commitment to physical force. The Fenian Michael Doheny (1805–63) claims in *The Felon's Track* (1849) that he and Davis had designed the tactic of the meetings 'to train the country people to military movements and a martial tread' which sounds more like a line from a *Nation* ballad than a sober tactic. It need no more be taken literally than

O'Connell's 'Mallow Defiance' when after a dinner on 11 June in the County Cork town he cried, 'We were a paltry remnant in Cromwell's time. We are nine million now.'

The baiting brinkmanship continued. A meeting was called for Sunday 8 October at Clontarf, remembering the glories of Brian the brave, that was to make Tara look 'like a caucus'. On the Saturday evening, when in those days of difficult journeys many would have already started for the venue, Peel proscribed the meeting. Already there were warships in Dublin Bay and troops of artillery at Clontarf. O'Connell had to decide quickly and he called off this most prestigious of meetings. Though this was not the end of the Liberator nor yet of the association it was realised that a turning point had been reached. Repeal was not to be achieved by passive meetings, however monstrous, and Peel, the old adversary, had won. The government did what it could to save O'Connell's reputation by sending him to prison for a year. He was now sixty-nine and already suffering from the intermittent senility that made his last years so pitiful. True, after three months he was released from Richmond Gaol where he had been more honoured guest than convict, but his career was over. His last speech in the House, made on 8 February 1847, was almost inaudible but accurate in its grisly prophecy:

> Ireland is in your hands . . . your power. If you
> do not save her she can't save herself . . . I
> predict . . . that one quarter of the population
> will perish unless you come to her relief.

Daniel O'Connell died in Genoa on 15 May on his way to Rome. There his heart lies. His body is buried in Glasnevin in the 'Great Comedian's tomb', in Yeats's not-inaccurate description. He more than anyone recreated Ireland and gave the lost and hopeless masses heart and hope. He taught them democracy and gave them all the means to fight for themselves. Those means were not always to be the ones he would have preferred, but without him the process from eighteenth-century disarray to twentieth-century expertise would have been certainly slower. The climbdown over Clontarf was the correct and humane decision at the time, but it did raise the question about what message he intended the mass meetings to send. To Mitchel it was 'war in our time', and they certainly paved the way for Fenianism and the IRB. Yet their failure did not mean that all constitutional methods would fail; merely that the gathering together of many thousands of people to fancy they were listening to the voice of their leader had reached the end of its usefulness. As a Benthamite, practicality was O'Connell's dominant trait and it seemed that involvement of the whole nation was the key to success. His acquiescence in the death of the Irish language simply replicated the country's practice and the utilitarian appeal was unanswerable. Characteristically he found Biblical precedent:

> A diversity of tongues is no benefit; it was first imposed upon mankind as a curse, at the building of Babel . . .

but he used his own Gaelic eloquence when it was appropriate.

O'Connell had many faults and later patriots with smaller achievements have felt able to denigrate him. He brought priests into politics but for the most utilitarian of reasons: they were to be his teachers and his local organisers, and they would have more immediate authority than any other man in the parish. With the national schoolteachers (a bonus from the Drummond years) they ran the Reading Rooms that turned a population of illiterates into one with perhaps too much respect for education. He could be nauseating, by today's standards, with his bleating about 'the dear little Queen', and was far too public a Catholic for the taste of some Young Irelanders. His two great errors were affiliation with the Whigs and his total lack of *rapprochement* with the northern Protestants. His shade will no doubt scoff at the first and lecture about the total impossibility of dealing with Tories, especially Peel. Yet he should have sensed that Whigs (and their Liberal and Socialist heirs) were, as far as Ireland is concerned, inveterately pusillanimous in accepting the logic of their reforms; they tend to bow before the military establishment and have made little attempt to understand the quarter of the country's population that marches to different, usually Lambeg, drummers. When some historian a hundred years hence comes to write the history of Ireland up until his time he may well find that an ounce of Tory, unpopular decisions made, will always be worth a kilo of Liberal good intentions.

O'Connell rarely travelled north of Monaghan and his Belfast venture in January 1841 to sell Repeal was a disaster, not because he was not welcomed warmly by the growing population of Catholics but because he did not tangle with his adversary 'My friend Bully Cooke, the cock of the North' and had very few Protestants in his audiences. The usual 'spontaneous' street protests were arranged and two thousand dragoons and police were drafted in to prevent 'counter arrays'. The visit lasted barely four days and the Catholics, who had borne the brunt of the reprisals when Jack Lawless, one of O'Connell's most active lieutenants, had promised 'an invasion of Ulster' in 1828, were greatly relieved. O'Connell's failure to make an attempt at understanding the Unionist north has been shared by nearly all nationalist leaders since. In most aspects of his career he was very much a child of his time (except that, unlike the racist Mitchel, he was sternly against the slave trade and the southern United States), but there was more than a fleeting wisp of glory about his time and it was he who generated what glory there was.

11

Farm and Factory

When Grattan in his famous speech against the Act of Union described Ireland as 'in her tomb, helpless and motionless', he was using the elegantly formal Augustan rhetoric of his time. It was a description much more apt for the country at the time of the Liberator's death. The 'nine million' of his Mallow defiance had been reduced by starvation, disease and emigration to six and a half. By the time of the 1861 census the figure was 5.7 million and the downward tendency would continue. The long forecast cataclysm had happened but it was much worse than even the wisest prophet guessed. A fungal infection partially destroyed the potato crop in 1845 and totally in 1846. For a large portion of the rural population the potato with milk had provided a well-balanced high-energy diet with a nice proportion of carbohydrates, proteins and minerals. Those who subsisted on it exclusively were reckoned to consume a stone a day, which meant an intake of a million potatoes in a life of fifty years, the modal expectancy figure for the period.

Peel, for all of O'Connell's detractions, knew Ireland

well. He had been MP for Cashel and chief secretary from 1812 to 1816. He was an efficient administrator and had obviated the worst effects of the 1817 famine by providing £250,000 for relief. In 1846 he authorised the purchase of £100,000 worth of maize for distribution to prevent food prices from rising and provided £365,000 to subsidise the work of local committees. He did serious harm to his party by abolishing the Corn Laws in an attempt to provide cheaper bread. The potato crop was the only one that was affected. Wheat and corn harvests were as good as ever and though imports of corn were greater than exports it was clear that it was actually being exported from a country where a third of the population was starving and in danger of death.

The Tory government fell in June 1846 and Lord John Russell became the leader of a minority Whig administration. He was firmly non-interventionist, a fervent disciple of the current doctrine of *laissez faire*, when it was regarded as not only wrong but futile for governments to interfere with inexorable economic laws. No money was to be made available for relief, but 'relief works', largely pointless schemes such as building walls or roads which led nowhere, which were to be financed entirely from the rates. The chief 'villains' in this policy were Sir Charles Trevelyan, Assistant Secretary to the Treasury and Charles Wood, Chancellor of the Exchequer. Trevelyan was a believer in Malthus's theories concerning the impossibility of raising the standards of a depressed class because all amelioration would be nullified by a consequent rise in the population of the class. In a particularly unctuous way, he and many like him saw the

Irish hunger as God's way of solving the problem. 'The great evil with which we have to contend is not the physical evil of the famine but the moral evil of the selfish, perverse and turbulent character of the people.' This in description of a people who with rare exceptions allowed food trains to pass unhindered to the ports for shipment! It was statements like this that enabled Mitchel to cry, 'The Almighty, indeed, sent the potato blight, but the English created the Famine.'

The pictures in the *Illustrated London News* of ragged people searching for healthy potatoes, of famine funerals, soup kitchens, evictions and emigrant ships have left a permanent impression of misery. If folk memory of coffins with sliding bottoms, roads heaving with hungry people barely able to walk, mass graves and the potent superstition of the hungry grass is added to this it is easy to understand how the famine years seem to be with the Irish still. Figures like 932,000 people maintained in workhouses in 1849, 100,000 emigrants bound for Canada (the most economical route to the States) in 1847, 3,000,000 people a day being fed in government soup kitchens (even the Whigs had to come to their humane senses in the end) in the August of that same year, 104,000 tenants evicted in 1850, eventually become incomprehensible. Easier to empathise with the despair of the many who shut the doors of their hovels and quietly died.

Not all the country was stricken equally. East Ulster and Leinster were affected least because of their mixed husbandry, though they were not free of the epidemics of typhus and relapsing fever, and the cholera which appeared in the later stages of the visitation. The Society of Friends emerge as the heroes of the period, providing relief and in spite of appalling conditions getting it to the places of greatest need. It was their success that forced the government to acquiesce in a change of tactic, substituting direct action for 'hands-off'. Those evangelical agencies which had during the 1830s set up proselytising experiments, such as Nangle's 'village' in Dugort, on Achill, and Gayer's in Dingle continued with their mixture of bread and sermons. The offering of food to the starving in exchange for conversion still sounds reprehensible, however worthy and sincere the personalities involved or the perceived spiritual advantage accruing to those who saw the light. Certainly the charge of 'souperism' is still a bitter one although, like several other aspects of the cataclysm, the myth outdistances the facts. When the Catholic Church, led by Archbishop Paul Cullen, confident, well-manned and full of a post-apocalyptic fervour, attempted to reclaim the handful of lost souls, they were not reticent in their condemnation. The charges of soup-taking that were levelled at certain families for at least a hundred years were never disavowed and often perpetuated by pastors.

It would have been strange if the Church had not capitalised on the shock of the Biblical catastrophe, playing up a sense of visitation by a rampant Jehovah as a punishment for sin. The fact that he was very selective in his doom did not matter, since it was difficult for the inhabitants of one part of a country to have information about places even a score of miles away. The effect was to create a docile laity for a clergy that were entering upon their period of greatest power and influence. Most of the priests were Maynooth-trained and the tenor of its practice reflected the views of a very strict, supposedly Jansenistic teaching staff. The sense of unworthiness, of the extreme difficulty of the ordinary mortal's ever being able to merit grace, made reception of the sacraments a rare event, and even children were regarded as sinners. The sense of guilt that pastors encouraged their flocks to feel was not dishonest; they felt it too, and the sins that were the most dreaded and most shocking were those concerning sex. Seven other commandments, especially the ones about false witness and neighbour's property, seemed by comparison to be discounted, and the fifth about killing was always going to be problematic among a population that was by reason of conquest instinctively 'agin the guvment'.

Most of the demographic changes associated with post-Famine Ireland had their beginnings before the 1840s. Emigration was well established, though the destinations were usually to the east, to Scotland, northern England and southern Wales rather than the United States. In the 1840s, America became a chimerical promised land. The curve of early marriages that was so characteristic of the poorer rural population for a century before had flattened out by the 1830s. By 1850 the days of reckless subdivision of properties were over. Farms were larger and tended to mix tillage and livestock. The holding had to be preserved and younger sons and daughters were obliged to find alternative sources of living. (The quarter of a million that emigrated annually from 1847 were the eugenic cream of the country, the source of the burgeoning population before the catastrophe.) The heir bided his time and rarely married before the age of thirty. Marriages had clearly materialist elements and young women had to be in possession of a 'fortune' before they were considered marriageable.

The Famine permanently seared the psyche of those whom it affected, notably the million who survived by fleeing. They brought with them a hatred of England, blaming the coloniser unjustly for deliberate genocide. The numbers who took with them a picture of a ruined land had swollen to three million by 1870. They also had memories of vile treatment on the 'coffin' ships, unseaworthy hulks that were pressed into service for quick profits and braved the North Atlantic with a complement of which less than three-quarters had any chance of survival. One noted philanthropist, Vere Foster, travelled on such a ship, the *Washington*, in 1850, so that he might write the report that led to minimum standards being set for such transports. His subscription of £10,000 of his own money to assist passages was the best way he felt he could help alleviate the suffering. The land could no longer sustain its teeming population so exodus was the only solution. By 1900 four million Irish had crossed the Atlantic and after initial privations and denigration had become a significant factor in east-coast (and mid-west) local and national politics. From 1850 onwards America was to be the source of money and succour for all native nationalist movements.

If 'England' was execrated for its apparent attempted genocide, an equally imprecise class, that of 'landlords', was only a little lower down on the hate register. No official figures were kept until 1849, but police records show that during the following five years, 250,000 people were formally and permanently evicted from their holdings. Evidence shows that it was farmers, many of whom were Catholic, who treated the needy worst of all, bringing cases against wretches who stole turnips, for example, and disapproving of the magistrates' clemency. This is the class that objected to any suggestion of banning grain exports. Many landlords, in fact, bankrupted themselves in their attempts to care for their needy tenants; others, they who gained the lasting reputation for their class, ignored the plight of their dependants and made sure of their rents. The 'clearances' which an agronomic diagnosis would have recommended were carried out by death, emigration and eviction. The restoration of tilled lands to grass for livestock required clearance and in many cases rents were racked not for income but for 'legal' eviction. The lately congested districts of the south and west were now empty and the pattern of life in rural Ireland was fundamentally changed. (The rocky settlements along the coasts from Malin Head to Kinsale continued to be overpopulated, their denizens subsisting on restored potatoes, sea produce – pollack for the table, lobster and kelp for sale – and seasonal migrant labour, and became the concern of Balfour's Congested Districts Board, universally known as the CDB, that was set up in 1890.)

Emigration from the four 'loyal' counties of Derry, Antrim, Down and Armagh, though not unknown, was only a fraction of that from the rest of the country. (The favoured destination was Canada, which many of the Scots 'kith and kin' had made their new home ever since the 1745 débâcle and the clearances that followed; the Ulster emigration made Toronto a city as 'Irish' as Boston if not as 'Fenian'.) The region was different in many respects: it had the greatest concentration of Protestants, including more than 90 per cent of all Presbyterians. The system of landholding was different: the 'Ulster custom' gave tenants a greater security of tenure and the plantation legacy was of many small wholly owned farms. The region had, too, established a reputation for industry (and industriousness) from the middle of the eighteenth century and survived the change from cottage to factory and the meteoric rise and fall of cotton. It had not only accepted the Union but realised that its prosperity, rather precarious as it turned out, was a function of that coupling. It was able to overcome its insularity, in an age of cheap, if stormy, sea transport, and Belfast grew like Birmingham into a recognisable Victorian industrial city. It partook of the advantages of the Industrial Revolution, such as they were, in a way that Dublin and Cork could not, even if they had wished, aspire to.

The region had no more in the way of 'natural resources' than the rest of the country, but it could attract investment and was lucky in the entrepreneurial interest that was shown in it by men of genius. It was conscious of the revolutionary changes that made Britain the world leader in heavy industry. The industrial canal that was built in 1742 was the first in what was not yet legally the United Kingdom. It was cut from Lough Neagh to Newry to convey the coal from Brackaville (later Coalisland) to the sea. The generation of one industry by the requirements of another, a recurring characteristic of the industrial society, may be seen in the way that engineering, which was developed to maintain the large linen mills, became an important industry in its own right. Ropeworks, factories for bacon, tobacco, aerated mineral water factories (the last popular in a province which valued temperance), iron foundries became the most obvious features of the Lagan valley. The commercial reputation of the other northern city was founded on shirt-making, which survived as a profitable undertaking for a hundred years and gave Derry a skewed economy in that the women were in full employment. Derry, too, was noted for processed pork, tobacco manufacture (the Gallaher whose huge Belfast factories made a walk down York Street a plunge into passive smoking began his trade in Sackville Street in Derry's city centre) and its shipyard. The graving dock was to prove important during World War II when Derry was the Allied La Rochelle.

Belfast's greatest industrial fame rests in her shipbuilding, though again there was no necessary reason why Dargan's Island should have become one of the world's leading yards. The site was artificially created by William Dargan, the father of Irish railways, when he built the Carrickfergus line. The Ritchie brothers had founded a shipyard at the Old Lime Kiln Dock in 1791 and the famous firm of Harland and Wolff completed its first ship, the *Khersonese*, sixty years later. The real genius of the firm, William Pirrie, became chairman in 1895, and what is taken to be the first modern liner, the White Star Line flagship *Oceanic*, was launched in

1899. The firm's reputation grew: the *Olympic* was ready in 1910 and the 'unsinkable' *Titanic* was launched and lost in 1912, a financial and symbolic blow to the company. The success of Harland and Wolff encouraged the setting up of other firms, notably Workman and Clark, which was established in 1880.

As ever, reputation was more important than natural resources. None of the enterprises that were Belfast's pride were established by native Ulstermen, the nearest in blood being the Canadian Pirrie whose parents had been Ulster emigrants. As far as the entrepreneurs were concerned the Union was a literal fact; they were actively Unionist and on the whole preferred a Protestant workforce. (Pirrie was a supporter of Home Rule second; business was business.) George Smith Clark was notably anti-Catholic and employed them only by default. (When the Northern Ireland state was in its birth throes in 1920 he led the agitation for the sacking of all Catholics, not only from the shipyard but from all heavy industries.) Indeed they were on sufferance everywhere and their treatment at work was a reliable gauge of the current political temperature. They were needed as hewers of wood and drawers of water and thronged to the city, and, but not in significant numbers to the satellite towns of Lisburn, Carrickfergus, Newtownards and Bangor. Sectarian violence was endemic from 1850 on, the moment it became clear that because of the Famine and more normal demographic factors there was a sizeable population of Papists, Taigs or Fenians (the latest and most adhesive label) within the city boundary; after 1850 occupancy meant franchise.

The riots were seasonal in times of peace but when anti-Home Rule agitation was at its height the season was open. The danger to Catholics was considerable because they were very much a minority and though the RIC (granted the prefix in 1867 in recognition of their 'defeat' of the Fenians) were on the whole a non-partisan, if armed, force, the Town police, the first line of peacekeepers, consisted almost entirely of Orangemen. The industrialists were in general against the idea of Home Rule in any form, not because of the Rome Rule equation, but because they doubted a Dublin parliament's total commitment to the technically larger city and because they knew that agitation unsettled the workforce. Whenever the threat of a modification to the 1801 act loomed large, exigency plans for the transfer of business to the Clyde or the Mersey were taken out and dusted. The industrialists may not have heard Henry Cooke's speech on 21 January 1841 when he cried, 'Look at [the prosperity] of Belfast and be a Repealer – if you can,' but they surely assented to it.

Yet the Union had failed; it was unthinkable that even the smugly self-righteous pair, Trevelyan and Wood, would have been non-interventionist if the Famine had raged in Derbyshire or Dundee. That they could take in their stride gross slum poverty in British cities was clear from Dickens's shortest and most coldly satirical novel *Hard Times* (1854), but a death toll of three quarters of a million . . . All excuses damned the Union more deeply: lack of awareness of the extent of the problem; difficulties of bringing relief; lack of cooperation from the landowners and the exacerbation of the problem by eviction – would these conditions have obtained with a Dublin parliament? With the passing of the 1850 franchise act, the group of nationalist MPs, once called O'Connell's 'tail', was enough with the right leverage to wag the dog. O'Connell had taught the techniques of tactical voting and procedural obstructionism; with eighty-five members in the 'tail' in 1885 (the increase due to the 1884 extension of the franchise, the 'mud-cabin' act, which tripled the Irish electorate to three-quarters of a million) Joe Biggar was able to make it a very effective parliamentary instrument. It was clear that Repeal, the great word of the 1840s, would inevitably be obtained. The ultimate supremacy of two-thirds of the population that owed no allegiance to Britain was unquestioned. The one-third who had, they thought, nothing to gain by independence would in time, it was sanguinely believed, see where their best advantage lay.

In the meantime the 'attempted genocide' had to be avenged, or so it seemed to the more stridently self-conscious heirs of Young Ireland; and the question of the land had to be settled. The two issues were to be inter-connected. Many of Smith O'Brien's associates in the failed rising of 1848 had escaped to France or America and continued with revolutionary zeal undiminished to plan for the physical force option which they believed was the only means of making Britain concede independence. In 1858, ten years after Ballingarry, John O'Mahony (1816–77) suggested to James Stephens (1825–1901) the foundation of a new republican organisation, at first known as the the Irish Revolutionary Brotherhood and later as the Irish Republican

Brotherhood. Stephens was to organise at home, while O'Mahony would be in charge of the American arm. Because of their stoicism in imprisonment, their dominance of the English media during the 1860s and their requisition by Pearse as revolutionary icons, the names of O'Donovan Rossa, John Devoy, T. C. Luby, Charles Kickham, Michael Doheny, John O'Leary and Michael Davitt are still entities in an emotional hall of fame. They were soon called 'Fenians' after the Fianna of Fionn Mac Cumhaill in the saga, the name originating in New York.

The movement, unusually for Irish ventures of the kind, found its main membership mainly in working-class men, largely Catholic, who were prepared to run the gauntlet of Church disapproval. Archbishop Cullen (made Cardinal in 1866) was a particularly high profile administrator and entirely in agreement with the papacy in his abomination of revolutionary movements. He organised an Irish brigade to assist the papal troops in their defence of Pio Nono against Garibaldi's Red Shirts. The IRB had its organ in the *Irish People,* a rather more energetic and specific paper than the *Nation* and edited by Kickham, who later wrote *Knocknagow* (1879), Ireland's most popular nineteenth-century novel. The first opportunity for a show of public strength was the bringing home of the body of the old 1848 warrior Terence Bellew MacManus, who died on 15 January 1861 in San Francisco. The Fenian chapter there had the coffin exhumed and it began a long, long journey home. Cullen forbade a lying in state in Dublin's Pro-Cathedral, so when the body reached Dublin on 4 November it was placed in the

Mechanics Institute (in a later incarnation to be the first Abbey Theatre). The funeral on the following Sunday was huge, and made a considerable but significant detour by Thomas Street where Emmet had been executed fifty-eight years before. Even Luby, who had organised the event, was astounded by the size of the crowd. At the graveside in Glasnevin a panegyric was preached in defiance of Cullen by Fr Thomas Lavelle, the Mayo priest, who was later accused of clerical intimidation at the Galway election of 1872. The direct descendants of the Fenians were to stage exactly the same kind of emotional event when Pearse made his famous 'Fenian dead' oration over the grave of O'Donovan Rossa on 1 August 1915.

Both were intended as preliminaries to a rising, but Stephens, who loved the idea of a secret society with its cells and oaths, was a notable procrastinator, and the 1865 insurrection – which was to be the more effective because of arms and trained men from America and timed to take place on 20 September, the anniversary of Emmet's rising – had to be aborted. On 15 September the *Irish People* was suppressed and O'Leary, Luby and Rossa were arrested. The turn of Stephens and Kickham came on 11 November, and John Devoy who took over command from Stephens was imprisoned the following February. Prison conditions were made deliberately harsh and Kickham's health was broken after he had served four of his fourteen years' penal servitude. O'Donovan Rossa, Devoy, O'Leary, Luby all served at least five years before being released on condition of exile. Stephens had escaped from Richmond Gaol a fortnight after his arrest with help from a warder who was a sworn Fenian brother. The fact that the movement had members in the army, police and prison service was balanced by the inevitable presence of informers.

The IRB had gained grudging respect, and its activities, apart from a few uncoordinated and short-lived affrays in Kerry, Louth, Wicklow, Tipperary, Cork, Limerick and Clare in March 1867, consisted mainly of attempted rescues of members. On 11 September Thomas Kelly and Timothy Deasy, now heads of the movement, were arrested in Manchester and one week later in a successful rescue attempt from a prison van in Manchester a police sergeant called Charles Brett was accidentally shot. Three Fenians, Philip Allen, Michael Larkin and Michael O'Brien were tried for his murder and hanged on 23 November. It was an age of instant ballads and 'God Save Ireland', which told of the 'gallant three' forever known as the 'Manchester Martyrs', attained almost the status of a national anthem. It was written by T. P. Sullivan for the *Nation,* now owned by his brother, A. M. Sullivan. Its tune was that of the American military march 'Tramp, Tramp, Tramp'. This was entirely appropriate, since it was the plan of such American Fenians as Thomas Meagher to use men trained in the Civil War to make the IRB an effective, disciplined and well-armed force. Many of his specially picked men were killed in Civil War battles, and internal dissension among American Fenians prevented the promised arms being sent in time for a 1865 rising. The other Fenian incident of 1867, the attempt to rescue Richard Burke and Joseph Casey from Clerkenwell

Detention Centre, was bungled and horrific. The charge was much too heavy; twelve people were killed instantly and of 138 seriously injured a further eighteen died. The prisoners did not escape – if they had been where they were thought to be they too would have been killed. The effect on the British public was predictable and a new and heady idea had been added to the 'protest' thinking of a section of the IRB. It was one that was unfortunately and pointlessly to persist.

The 'bold Fenian men' had for the time being been defeated. Factionalism followed and there were to be several localised eruptions organised by ever smaller splinter groups. A group significantly calling itself the 'Irish Republican Army' had invaded Canada at the end of May 1866. It was led by John O'Neill, a former Union general and Indian fighter who soon after his brief imprisonment abandoned further republican activity. One of the Fenian oaths started with the words: 'I do solemnly swear allegiance to the Irish Republic, *now virtually established* . . . '[emphasis mine]. This arrogation of sovereignty was to establish the moral right to carry on a war as if a country called the Republic of Ireland actually existed. It was a right later assumed by the IRA and so stated in 1920, 1938 and 1971. The 'Invincibles' who carried out the Phoenix Park murders of the chief and under-secretaries Lord Frederick Cavendish and Thomas Henry Burke on 6 May 1882 were another such 'independent' group. The undefined Fenian tradition lived on, regularly to reawaken the Phoenix Flame, as O'Donovan Rossa called the cause.

Apart from their mythology, which was accepted as a

legacy by other similar movements, the Fenians' most obvious successes were won more or less constitutionally in alliance with Parnell and the Irish Parliamentary Party, who brought the country within shouting distance of 'Home Rule'. The power of that solidarity was first seen in the Plan of Campaign, which was the first significant step in the process that was finally to settle the question of the ownership of the land of Ireland. From 1850 till 1880 there was a sense of stability, buoyancy even, in rural Ireland. That stability depended on emigration and such subsidies as the American letter, which was an important part of the homeside family's budget. Economic recession in the emigrants' destination meant an excess population at home, who often vented their frustration in the form of increased protest and unconstitutional activity. For most Irish farmers at this time rents were endurable (just), eviction unlikely and tenure tolerably secure. A majority had achieved the 'Three Fs' – fair rent, fixity of tenure and free sale – that Charles Gavan Duffy's Tenant Right League had sought in 1850.

Among landlords as ever it was the exceptions, the colourful personalities like Adair of Glenveagh, Lord Leitrim and poor Captain Boycott (who increased the vocabulary of social action much like the distant town of Coventry), whose names have been remembered, or kept alive by those for whom history is a weapon. Most were not at all like Michael Davitt's (1846–1906) emotional description of them as 'vampires'. Gladstone had begun to apply his political talents and moral authority to Irish affairs after a consideration of the causes of Fenianism and with a nudge from John Stuart

Mill towards the end of the 1860s. His 1870 Land Act was one of the first moves he made in his mission 'to pacify Ireland'. But he was unprepared for the efficiency of Davitt's Land League, which was formed soon after Davitt's return from America after serving seven years of his sentence for membership of the IRB. His hope of land nationalisation, a theory of his political mentor James Fintan Lalor (1807– 49), who had been Duffy's lieutenant in the 1845 agitation, was not to be realised, but it is to him and his judicious use of Parnell that the credit for the settling of the land question must be ascribed. His 1876 analysis showed that 70 per cent of the land was owned by fewer than 2,000 people, and three million small tenants and labourers owned no property at all.

The years 1879–81 saw a serious crisis in agriculture that seemed comparable with the Hungry Forties. Davitt organised the farmers of his native Mayo (he was the son of an evicted small tenant), exhorting them, 'Hold a firm grip of your homesteads and lands.' He persuaded Parnell to speak at his demonstrations and was able to provide the relief that was sorely lacking during the Great Famine with money provided by American Fenians, who had started calling themselves Clan na Gael in 1870. There was support from the Catholic clergy and the policy of ostracism was used most noisily in Lough Mask House, the home of Captain Boycott, when Lord Erne's crops were harvested by Cavan Orangemen at an astronomic cost. There were threats, special courts, independent collection of rents, agrarian outrages (2,500 in 1880 and 4,400 in 1881) and, when Parnell was arrested in October 1881, a rent strike. (Parnell was unabashed; he warned Gladstone, 'Captain Moonlight will take my place.')

Gladstone's Land Act of 1881 granted the Three Fs and the 'Healy Clause', ensuring that tenants' improvements would not be penalised by rent increases. By then, independence was the prize and the more austere of the Irish leaders were disinclined to spend further time on bread and butter issues like land ownership. It was under Conservative governments that the acts that enabled the Irish peasantry finally to purchase their farms were passed. On 14 August 1885, Lord Ashbourne's Purchase of Land Act provided loans that enabled a total of 942,600 acres to be purchased. Wyndham's Act (14 August 1903) all but completed the process and a further measure known as Birrell's Act (called after the engaging Chief Secretary) gave the CDB powers of compulsory purchase in December 1909, thus allowing even the poorest tenants to acquire the land they worked. By now the landlords were as anxious as the tenants to have done with the largely unprofitable lands, although they were able to manipulate the terms of the measures to sell their grand demesnes to the government and repurchase them at the same low mortgage rates as their late tenants. And so it stayed until land purchase became compulsory in 1920 and many landlords left for political as much as economic reasons.

The significant history of modern Ireland could be said without much exaggeration to have begun in the bad winters of 1879–81.

12

Home Rule – Rome Rule

Fenianism had predictable effects: thundering denunciation from the press and in parliament and a great deal of thought among those whose business it was to maintain the health of the body politic. John Stuart Mill (1806–73), the social reformer and philosopher who 'humanised' Bentham's utilitarianism (at its extreme point as savagely inhuman as *laissez faire*), stated in 1868 that the recurring question was not so much England's Irish problem as Ireland's English problem. In *England and Ireland* he opined to his English readers that there was 'no other nation of the civilised world, which, if the task of governing Ireland had happened to devolve upon it, would not have shown itself more capable of that work than England has hitherto done.' There was the usual uproar that greets any criticism of England: one Irish landlord said that Mill should be sent to gaol as a Fenian but Gladstone, who became Liberal prime minister for the first time in 1868, was moved to make Ireland the main business of the rest of his long parliamentary career.

His first move was to disestablish the Church of Ireland (on very generous terms) and incidentally initiate tenant ownership, in that the bill provided for the purchase of glebe lands. The 'pacification' of Ireland, Gladstone's stated intention, was going to imply more than just land reform. He began to consider what Ireland's new constitutional leader, Isaac Butt (1813–79), had tentatively named 'Home Rule'. Butt was a son of a Church of Ireland rector from Stranorlar, County Donegal who became professor of political economy at Trinity but left the academic life for the richer pickings of the bar in 1841. (The son of a widow from an early age, his finances were precarious for his whole life.) He became as famous a pleader as O'Connell, with whom he engaged in public debate as the voice of Protestant ascendancy. The Famine, especially the emotional scenes that he witnessed at ports of departure, had a profound effect on him, as had the demeanour of the nationalists he defended in the courts, notably Smith O'Brien and Meagher in 1848 and many Fenians in the 1860s. He sat as a Conservative MP for Youghal from 1852–65 but, having founded the Home Government Association in 1870, stood as a federal candidate for Limerick in 1871. By 1874 he was head of the Home Rule party, with fifty MPs at his control.

His gradualism and 'gentlemanly' constitutionalism were regarded as too radical for his Protestant friends and they exasperated Catholics. His lieutenant, the Protestant IRB Belfast MP, Joseph Gillis Biggar (1828–90), who represented Cavan 1874–90, was by House standards far from gentlemanly in that he used every procedural trick to bring it to a standstill. Butt was continually embarrassed by this obstruct-ionism and by Biggar's abrasive manner both in and out of the House. Biggar even named the Prince of Wales as a 'stranger' and forced him to leave the House. When Butt was effectively dismissed in 1879 by the rising star, Parnell, his disappointment was mitigated by the satisfaction of having initiated the process that would eventually lead to independence and by a reluctance to be associated with an increasingly 'ungentlemanly' campaign.

Charles Stewart Parnell (1846–91) was a Protestant landlord, who inherited the estate of Avondale in County Wicklow on the death of his father when he was thirteen. For a further sixteen years he led a fairly aimless life until his election as a Home Rule candidate for Meath in a by-election in 1875. His family had been anti-Union and pro-Emancipation and his mother, an American, was in opinions if not in action firmly anti-English. (Having an American mother had a liberalising effect on another player in the Irish comedy, Winston Churchill, though Jennie Jerome could not have been said to have affected the views of her husband, the Orange-card-playing Lord Randolph.) Parnell's cold and reserved exterior and laconic, almost monosyllabic, speech concealed a passionate nature. His noted dislike of the English was not unknown among his class and it is generally believed that slights inflicted at Cambridge, which he left without taking a degree, intensified it. His alliance with the Fenians was not one of peers, though a belief that he supported them, commonly held, especially in America, widened his command and brought in many subscriptions for party funds.

His arrest on 13 October 1881, along with the principal

leaders of the Land League, was the equivalent of graduation. From then on he was 'The Chief' and had the convenience of having most of his court with him in Kilmainham Gaol. The increase of rural violence led to a suspension of *habeas corpus*. Gladstone's policy was always to have some offensive coercion measure in place so that he could rescind it as proof of his sincerity. He concluded an agreement with Parnell, the intermediaries significantly being Captain and Mrs O'Shea, that was known as the 'Kilmainham Treaty'. The rent strike was called off and the Land Leaguers released on 2 May 1882. Parnell was now at the height of his power, and in the phrase of his adversarial colleague, Tim Healy (1855–1931), 'the uncrowned king of Ireland'. He was able to continue in spite of the horrific Phoenix Park murders and the government measures that followed, including the creation of a Special Irish Branch at Scotland Yard. (This was the forerunner of the modern Special Branch which deals with all aspects of political security.) He faced down accusations in *The Times* (18 April 1887), based on diaries forged by journalist Richard Pigott, that he not only condoned killings during the Land War but was actually implicated himself. He was finally cleared of all charges on 13 February 1890. The 'Thunderer' paid £5,000 in an out-of-court settlement of Parnell's libel action and lost forever its reputation for infallibility.

The election of 1885 returned eighty-six Irish Party MPs, T. P. O'Connor, who was afterwards for many years 'father of the House', representing the Scotland Division of Liverpool. Their numbers were exactly the difference between the Liberal 335 and the Conservative 249. On 8 April 1886 the seventy-six-year-old Gladstone announced a Home Rule Bill for Ireland. Its terms were modest, offering the kind of partial devolution that Craig and Carson accepted for 'Ulster' in 1921, powers internal and concerned with taxation, police, civil service and judiciary. It was defeated by thirty votes on its second reading on 8 June but not in time to stop a summer of rioting in Belfast in which thirty-two people were killed and 377 seriously injured. (The real number of dead was put at over fifty; not for the last time the true number of fatalities was concealed). The thought of a priest-ridden Dublin government was enough to set off volatile Belfast, especially when its Protestant population, both working class and bourgeois, had been inflamed by the brilliant demagoguery of the Rev Hugh Hanna who earned his nickname, 'Roaring', in the pulpit of St Enoch's Presbyterian Church. Parnell's response showed the same ignorance of the true nature of the Ulster Protestant resistance that had weakened O'Connell's leadership. In a speech at Plymouth on 26 June he suggested with less than full awareness of the situation that '1,000 men of the Royal Irish Constabulary will be amply sufficient to cope with all the rowdies that the Orangemen of the North can produce.'

Some of the blame for the trouble must be laid at Randolph Churchill's door. He was a clever but erratic politician and like most of the Conservative party convinced that any flaw in the well-wrought urn that was the British Empire would lead to its eventual dissolution. He also felt an obligation not to leave loyal Britishers to the mercies of a nationalist regime. Most of all he wanted to put the Conservatives back in power. In a letter to Lord Justice Fitzgibbon on 16 February 1866 he wrote:

> I decided some time ago that if the GOM ['grand old man'= Gladstone] went for Home Rule, the Orange card would be the one to play. Please God it may turn out to be the ace of trumps and not the two.

Churchill landed from the steamer at Larne on 26 February after an unusually rough crossing and declared: 'Ulster at the proper moment will resort to its supreme arbitrament of force. Ulster will fight, and Ulster will be right.' His immediate purpose was attained: a Conservative government under Lord Salisbury was returned on 25 July. The Orange card had not been necessary after all; Joseph Chamberlain had split from the Liberals to form the 'Unionist' party. Churchill knew Ireland well enough to state with a certain prophetic accuracy, 'Personal jealousies, government influences, Davitt, Fenian intrigue will all be at work, and the bishops who in their heart of hearts hate Parnell and don't care a scrap for home rule will complete the rout.'

Parnell was bitterly disappointed but knew that any measure of the sort would require an administration that could put the upper house in its place. He continued to lead his party and work for the improvement of his nationalist followers, though he tended to view with the gravest suspicion the reforms introduced by the Conservative administration of the kind that were later to be called 'killing Home Rule with kindness'. The land war rumbled on but Parnell was able to dissociate himself from Tim Harrington's Plan of Campaign, which signalled a new assault on landlordism. In February 1886 he had imposed the not very suitable candidate Captain O'Shea on the Galway by-election. Healy and Biggar were outraged and it was clear that most people knew what Biggar spoke aloud: 'The candidate's wife is Parnell's mistress and there's nothing more to be said.' It was true and had been the case for six years. Katharine O'Shea (the correct pronunciation of the name may be found in Healy's rasping jibe: 'O'Shea who must be obeyed') had borne Parnell three children between 1882 and 1884, clearly with the complaisance of the husband. O'Shea was known as a fairly feckless character and indeed his parliamentary career was, to say the least, disappointing. He did not sit with the other Irish Party members and voted against Home Rule!

Matters came to a head in 1889 when O'Shea filed for divorce on Christmas Eve, naming Parnell as co-respondent. The undefended suit was heard on 17 November 1890 and O'Shea was awarded custody of the children. Gladstone was not prepared to risk collaboration any longer with a party led by such a public sinner and the Catholic Church acted precisely as Churchill said they would. The party was split and would stay so until 1900. Moral indignation was not the main cause of the schism. Parnell was the 'uncrowned king' but his closest colleagues found him wilful, absent and arrogant. They were appalled at the risks he took and, at the protracted meeting held between 1 and 6 December in Committee Room 15 of the House, should have shown an able politician what he had to do. Cecil Rhodes, the Empire-builder with whom he had a quixotic friendship, had sent the prescription in a cable from Salisbury: 'Resign – marry – return.' Parnell had the embarrassment of seeing Justin McCarthy lead out forty-four now 'anti-Parnellite' MPs. He chose not to resign but to fight on with great courage. He and Katharine (neither of them used the name 'Kitty') were married at a registry office in Steynings, Surrey on 25 June 1891. Four months later he was dead. Once during the Home Rule campaign of 1866 rumours of his death had caused him to ask, 'What did I die of?' The cause on 6 October was almost certainly a coronary.

Parnell had taken the nation that O'Connell had lifted from the mud and made it a united force, thoroughly politicised. With Biggar in parliament and Davitt in the field he had presided over the solution of the land question and prescribed the remedy for Ireland's ill-worn colonialism. Unlike the Protestants of the North the Catholics of the rest of the country were far from docile; neither were they instinctively rebellious. Their innate conservatism had to be laid aside as a luxury to be worn again in peace. The greatest achievement of Parnell was that the 1880s became a decade of political unity and action, in contrast to the 1890s and the 1870s. His most serious flaw was his invincible ignorance about the Ulster Protestant temperament and the strange mixture of hubris and inertia that led to his downfall. He was a tragic hero lacking only a Sophocles or an Ibsen to explicate his true nature. He and O'Connell are the oddly different but still colossal figures that bestride the recuperative century.

In 1893, Gladstone tried to push through another Home Rule Bill, allowing for a more phased introduction of devolution than in 1886, and again it was passed by a margin of thirty-four votes but was thrown out by the Lords in September of that year. Of a total electorate of 460 only forty-one voted aye. On 2 March in the Ulster Hall in Belfast, a kind of lay temple of Protestant protest, William Johnston 'of Ballykilbeg', a noted Unionist and verbal extremist, carried a motion that Home Rule should be resisted passively. Agitation and intermittent rioting continued (the Orange definition of 'passive resistance'). A march of 100,000 loyalists was held on 4 April and Arthur Balfour, a future Conservative prime minister who had been chief secretary in 1887, joined Edward Saunderson, the founder of the Irish Unionist party, on the platform as the concourse passed the Linen Hall in the city centre. By now the Chief had been three years dead and the Irish Party was riven with factions and acrimonious accusations and counter-accusations. Home Rule was not to emerge again as an issue until Redmond had patched the party together and the 1911 Parliament Act had seriously weakened the Lords' veto.

The idea that the Irish Literary Renaissance was generated by a felt need to fill the political vacuum left by the fall of the Chief, and the miserable wrangling that followed, was largely an invention of Yeats, who saw himself as the equivalent literary chief. The last decade of the old century and the first of the new were remarkable in their cultural denseness. They also saw the foundation of Sinn Féin (originally Cumann na nGaedhael) and the Dungannon Clubs. As the name implied, the first was a separatist movement which even had an abstentionist candidate elected in 1908. Its founder was Arthur Griffith (1871–1922), and his approach was as much cultural as political. The advocacy of things Irish and disapproval of all English influences meant that he had strong fraternal links with the Gaelic League (founded in 1893); it also made his movement very sensitive to what it took to be criticism of any aspect of Irish life. He and his followers had no time for such ribald, earthy dramas as Synge's *In the Shadow of the Glen* (1903) and *The Playboy of the Western World* (1907). His literary mentor was Davis and he was able to tolerate any amount of inferior *Nation* poetry if he could advance Davis's recipe for an Irish Ireland. (He wrote a patriotic ballad himself called 'Twenty Men from Dublin Town'.) His goal was a country that could be independent while still having an allegiance to the British monarch. This policy, he believed, had enabled Hungary to break from Austria without leaving the empire. He hoped that the keeping of the personal link with the crown might reassure Ulster Protestants. It showed an awareness of political realities that was unusual among nationalist leaders, but he had forgotten the conditional nature of Ulster's loyalty. He did not fully realise that the northern Protestants felt themselves able, in order to prove their loyalty, to attack, and if necessary declare war on, the government to which they owed allegiance. Sinn Féin had a feminist element in that one of its ancillary bodies was Inghinidhe na hÉireann (The Daughters of Ireland), the women's movement set up by Maud Gonne (1866–1953) in 1900. The participation of women in national affairs began during the land agitation and they have played a full part in all aspects of them since.

The Dungannon Clubs were founded by Bulmer Hobson (1883–1969) and Dennis McCullough (1883–1968), both members of the IRB. The name was a gracious nod to the scene of the Ulster Volunteers 1782 convention. Hobson was a Quaker and, like Griffith, had worked as a printer. His magazine, the *Republic*, which was written by such brilliant (Protestant) journalists as Robert Lynd and James Wilder Good, was remarkably influential in spite of its short life (six months), and takes its place alongside the *Northern Patriot* and the *Shan Van Vocht* run by Alice Milligan and Ethna Carbery (Anna Johnston) as proof that Dublin did not have a monopoly of literary substitutes for parliamentary politics. Hobson was so little in awe of the guru of Coole and Abbey Street that on the train back to Belfast after a visit to Dublin, when he was humiliatingly refused permission to stage *Cathleen Ni Houlihan,* he said to his compartment companion, David Parkhill, 'Damn Yeats, we'll write our own plays,' and the Ulster Literary Theatre was born. It produced at least one significant playwright in Rutherford Mayne (the brother of Helen Waddell, the medieval scholar) and encouraged the work of the Ulster humorist, Leslie A. Montgomery, whose first pen-name was Lynn C. Doyle. Like Griffith, Hobson was against the 1916 Rising, believing in a policy of passive resistance and justifying the use of an armed force only for defence. He did his best to prevent the 'action of a small junta within the IRB' and was held incommunicado from the Good Friday till Easter Monday. His main writer, Robert Lynd, once the best known essayist of his day, whose father, sometime moderator of the Presbyterian Church, was the incumbent of the May Street church that had been built for Henry Cooke, was equally dismayed. Writing eighteen years after the rising in a tributary essay called 'Arthur Griffith: The Patriot' he insisted, ' . . . what brought the last insurrection to a successful issue was that, unlike all other Irish movements of the kind, it was based on or at least allied to the passive resistance movement of Arthur Griffith.'

The Gaelic League, founded by Douglas Hyde, a Roscommon son of the manse, and Eoin MacNeill, a law clerk from the Antrim Glens, was certainly as significant as the Irish Literary Theatre or the Abbey that was its successor. It did not spring fully grown from the Dagda's forehead but was the latest and most successful of a number of initiatives that had begun with the founding of the Royal Irish Academy in 1785. It had as precursors the Ossianic Society of 1853 and most significantly the Society for the Preservation of the Irish Language which was set up by David Comyn, a Protestant from County Clare, in 1876 and which afterwards, with the usual Irish amoebic tendency, split to form the Gaelic Union three years later. Hyde had come to notice with a public lecture delivered on November 1892: 'On the necessity for de-Anglicizing the Irish People'. The League was bound to gain the approval of Griffith, as it was explicitly separatist. Davis had advocated a revival of Irish and as a rejection of the imposed language of the colonial masters it was a most potent declaration of revolution. (James Joyce, one of the greatest Irish writers of the amazingly rich period, was moved neither by the League nor the Irish renaissance: he joined a League branch when he was at UCD but left when the teacher, Patrick Pearse (1879–1916), found it necessary to denigrate English and adduced one of Joyce's favourite words, 'thunder' as an example of its verbal inadequacy. As the most urban of writers Joyce did not feel much empathy with the Connacht Celtic Twilight.)

The League had twenty years of remarkable success largely because of the high motivation of its original members, its use of the Gaeltacht as a source of the living language and its understanding of the nature of adult education. It was non-sectarian at the start but soon Protestant members were made to feel unwelcome. One notable example was Canon J. O. Hannay, who as George A. Birmingham had written and was to continue to write more than fifty novels and plays, some serious, most hilarious and all acute in their observation of Irish life – *Benedict Kavanagh* (1907) was written in praise of the League; he was expelled in 1906. Hyde himself resigned in 1915 from an organisation which had become dominated by IRB members. The other association that became prominent at the time had no need to expel Protestants since it was sectarian from its beginning. The Gaelic Athletic Association had been founded in 1884 by Michael Cusack and Maurice Davin and was regarded from 1886 onwards by the Special Branch as an IRB association – with considerable justification. Even its first patron, Archbishop Thomas Croke, broke with the organisation in 1887 when he found a meeting 'packed to the throat with Fenian leaders'.

The period was, then, far from quiescent or politically inert. There had developed a significant Catholic middle class. By the turn of the century most of the dioceses had impressive cathedrals and junior seminaries, so called because they provided the necessary secondary education for future priests and were established by canonical rule. They also provided places for pupils who would form the educated Catholic laity, supplementing the work begun by such pioneers as Edmund Rice (1762–1844), whose order of Irish Christian Brothers (1820) had pioneered education for the sons of the Irish poor, and Catherine MacAuley (1778–1841), who founded the Sisters of Mercy (1831) with a mission that included nursing, social work and the education of girls. Protestants, especially those who lived in the hermetically sealed north, affected to believe that Catholics, especially the 'southerners', were dirty, feckless and unreliable. The only ones they had real experience of were the poor of Belfast, whose livelihood they constantly attacked as a matter of policy. They were notably incurious about the twenty-eight counties where they felt threatened but it is unlikely that if they had been adventurous enough to visit other parts in any numbers they could have failed to notice that the bourgeois Catholics of, say, Limerick or Cork were as prosperous, probably as conservative and certainly as respectable as the lordly ones who dwelt up the Malone

Road. They played tennis with the same vigour, were quite likely to be invited to army banquets, and took holidays in resorts as elegant and as decorously Victorian as Portrush or Bangor. It is still possible to see in places like Kilkee, Bray and Rosslare the archaeological remains of end-of-century 'watering places'. Golf, first played at the Curragh by a Scots regiment, became (and has remained) intensely popular, and the railways opened up the rugged beauties of Connemara, Kerry and Donegal to a growing tourist trade. It is a commonplace of history that the main interest of the Dublin populace on the Bank Holiday Monday of April 1916 was not in the shennanigans in the Post Office or Boland's Mills but in the usual Easter race meeting at Fairyhouse.

By 1900 John Redmond (1856–1918), the Wexford Parnellite, had managed to unite the Irish party and with great patience soothed its tendency to fragment under the maddening evasions of the Liberal administrations. When Asquith's Liberal government, in its anxiety to pass its welfare legislation, took on and defeated the House of Lords in 1910 it had to go to the country twice. The Liberals' overall majority of 1906 had so shrunk as to leave them dependent again on Redmond's restored Parnellites. It was clear that it was only a matter of time before Redmond brought in a Home Rule bill that could only be delayed by the Lords. This sent alarm signals ringing round Belfast. The *Ne Temere* decree of Pius X (1908) had convinced Irish Protestants that their street-cry, 'Home Rule, Rome Rule' was an exact statement of the case. Until then mixed marriages were fairly common, inevitable in the mixed nature of Ulster demography, especially in the west of the province. It was clearly unfair that the hated Vatican should set the terms for the marriage of partners of different faiths. One notorious case, as ever taken as the norm and not a terrible exception, confirmed what Protestants claimed to see as the proof of their worst dread. When in 1910 a Catholic Belfastman called McCann left his Protestant wife and took his children with him, he had public Church approval. Protestant freedom, religion and laws were threatened and, as Churchill had enunciated, Ulster would fight.

The cause of Irish Unionism was taken up by Bonar Law, who had replaced Arthur Balfour as head of what was now officially known as the Conservative and Unionist party. He had two very powerful Irish allies in James Craig (1871–1940) and the Dublin barrister Edward Carson (1854–1935) who felt, each with a slightly different attitude, that Dublin should not rule Belfast. Carson was a true supporter of the Act of Union and was conscious of no dissonance in being Irish and British. Craig, the son of a rich Ulster distiller, was not so idealistic, and had already begun to formulate the idea of a separate Ulster state that was to prove at least temporarily acceptable to everybody except the northern Catholics. They knew that they would be used as a kind of ballast and subject to much more subtle penal practices than those of Queen Anne's reign. As ever obedient and seamless in their solidarity, the Protestants began the necessary preparations that would lead to 'the arbitrament of force'. As at other times when the terrors of Home Rule were expressed, drilling and manoeuvres began. Orange, Black and Apprentice Boys lodges were quickly turned into a recruiting network for the Ulster Volunteer Force which was to be effectively armed with 35,000 German rifles landed 'illegally' (but with police connivance) at Larne, Bangor and Donaghadee in April 1914.

The Third Home Rule bill was introduced on 11 April 1912, proposing much the same terms as Gladstone's 1886 bill. The reaction in Ulster was much stronger. 28 September 1912 was designated Ulster Day and 218,000 men pledged themselves in solemn league and covenant 'to use all means to defeat the present conspiracy . . .' The bill was passed by the Commons on 16 January 1913 and thrown out with the usual vigour by the Lords, passed again in July and again dismissed. By the terms of the 1911 Parliament Act the Lords could now only delay the bill. Redmond seemed about to achieve what his uncrowned hero had failed to effect. The bill was finally carried on 25 May 1914. Already the army had signalled its non-cooperation in the Curragh Incident of 20 March, when General Gough persuaded fifty-seven out of seventy officers to resign their commissions rather than enforce Home Rule in Ulster. Carson and Craig were clearly kept informed of all developments by members of the High Command. Already the Liberal War Office, it seemed, was in danger of losing control of the armed forces. A bitter civil war seemed certain, with the prospect of 23,000 armed and exultant men ready to face down 1,000 soldiers and a now demoralised police force. With typical attention to detail, plans for the evacuation of civilians and a design for an Ulster currency had been approved. The means of permitting individual counties to opt out was included in Asquith's bill and the Lords successfully amended it to permit nine counties, not specified, to disregard it. Partition had been given respectability, but a conference called by George V, assumed to be on the side of the 'disloyalists', and which was held at Buckingham Palace in July 1914, failed to determine the nature of the separate state.

The situation was defused by the German invasion of Belgium on 4 August and Britain's immediate declaration of war. Redmond and Carson vied in their enthusiasm for recruitment and a band of Irish Volunteers matched the UVF. The Protestants, compliant to charismatic leadership, joined up in their thousands. They were granted the honour of belonging to a specially named Ulster Division and of marching to their deaths at the Ancre, a tributary of the Somme, in July 1916. In the first two days of the slaughter five and a half thousand were killed. Their Catholic brothers, who had joined in even greater numbers, had been, on the whole, motivated by bread and butter concerns. Wives and children would be much better fed by army pay than by unemployment benefit. Of 200,000 Irishmen who joined, 60,000 never returned. Protestants and Catholics are represented almost equally in both these statistics.

Though by common consent the implementation of the Home Rule bill had been shelved 'until the end of hostilities', the fate of Ulster had already been decided by Lloyd George. Counties Derry, Antrim, Down and Armagh were certain to be part of a region which would not be governed by

Dublin. What was still to be decided was the fate of Derry City, Tyrone, Fermanagh and bits of Donegal, Monaghan and Cavan – the Lords' amendment had catered for a nine county opt-out. Carson resigned from the war administration in January 1918 when he realised that Lloyd George intended to implement Asquith's bill; and the peace was to show that, in Winston Churchill's words, after the world deluge the falling waters would reveal 'the dreary steeples of Fermanagh and Tyrone emerging once again'. Partition was to be the logical answer to the faulted nature of the island of Ireland.

13

Fights for Freedom

The Ireland of the early twentieth century had a middle class externally indistinguishable from that in Britain but she also had in her cities some of the worst slums in Europe. Dublin, especially, was notorious and even contemporaries knew how bad conditions were. More than 100,000 people lived in one-room tenements, often in the degraded Georgian dwellings of the city's golden age of architecture, without water, light or sanitation. Unemployment was high, wages low and tuberculosis rife. Children were undernourished and hunger was general. The infant mortality rate of 2.76 per cent was the highest of all Western cities. The corporation had been in nationalist hands for at least ten years but there were no plans for urban renewal. Indeed it was discovered that sixteen Irish party councillors were slum landlords. With all attention fixed on British perfidy there was no policy either among politicians or the Church of social improvement. (Individual clergy and many religious orders did great work of charity but the hierarchy were and would continue to be suspicious of secular or state welfare schemes.)

The founding of the Irish Transport and General Workers

Union by the fiery Jim Larkin (1876–1947) in 1909 led to a rapid improvement in conditions for its members. Larkin was born in Liverpool and, like his Scots lieutenant James Connolly (1869–1916), retained, especially in passion, his native accent. Connolly was a socialist and his Irish Citizen Army (ICA) had been set up as a kind of rapid response force to protect pickets during the great six months' lockout of 1913. This was the employers' response to Larkin's success and it was led by W. M. Murphy (1844–1919), the transport tycoon. He was a noted member of the Irish party and required a written undertaking from workers that they would not join a union. Griffith, the Church and all but the members of the newly active IRB were publicly against Larkinism, as the labellers called union activity.

Connolly's brand of personal Marxism led him to commit his ICA, with their starry plough banner, to armed insurrection. He was later privy to the inner councils of Pearse and MacNeill, who had responded to the formation of the UVF by founding the Irish Volunteer Force at the Rotunda Rink on 25 November 1913. Their gunrunning, a trivial affair compared with the *Clyde Valley* cargo, was responded to rather differently. 1,500 guns were landed by the *Asgard* (navigated by Erskine Childers) at Howth on 26 July 1914 and the returning troops of the King's Own Scots Borderers (as a Scots regiment, more cordially detested than any English one), having failed to impound the guns, fired on a crowd at Bachelor's Walk, killing four and wounding thirty-seven. The genial chief-secretary, Augustine Birrell, (who resigned over Easter Week) sacked the Assistant-

Commissioner of the DMP, thus losing yet more friends among the local unionists, and the country was not slow to notice how different the reaction to the UVF gun running had been.

The IRB had been rekindled by the old Fenian Thomas J. Clarke (1857–1916) who had, at the age of fifty, been sent to Dublin by John Devoy (1842–1928), the king over the water, head of Clan na Gael in New York. His tobacconist shop in what is now Parnell Street became the nerve centre of his operations and by 1915 an armed rising was in plan. As ever, 'England's difficulty' was to be 'Ireland's opportunity'. The supreme council had Clarke, Sean MacDermott (1884–1916), Eamonn Ceannt (1881–1916) and Pearse (1879–1916). The latter three were prominent members of the now highly politicised Gaelic League. The late colonial administrator Roger Casement (1864–1916), also sponsored by John Devoy, went to Berlin to look for possible members of an Irish Brigade to be formed from prisoners of war, but without success. The IRB was in fact a tiny organisation, although there were cells in most parts of the country. Connolly's publicly expressed determination to lead his ICA in an insurrection was enough to have him incorporated in the war council lest his public utterances might lead to a serious tightening of security.

The date was fixed for Easter Monday, 24 April 1916, against the advice of most members of the Irish Volunteers and of Casement, who felt that no move should be made without a substantial number of German troops. The arms that were to come in the German ship, the *Aud*, were lost when the captain scuttled her on arrest by a British naval patrol in Tralee Bay on 21 April, and Casement, landing at Banna Strand, near Fenit in County Kerry, with instructions to cancel the rising, was arrested. MacNeill, after many misgivings, first approved then vetoed the venture, and cancelled all the planned synchronous sympathetic local outbreaks. In the end about 1,600 men, including 300 members of the ICA, occupied various buildings in Dublin, famously the General Post Office. Pearse read a proclamation entitled *The Proclamation of the Government of the Irish Republic to the People of Ireland* from the steps of the GPO. They held out until the Saturday when Pearse surrendered to General Lowe. (The commandant in Boland's Mills, Éamon de Valera (1882–1975), the mathematics lecturer who was to survive the executions, was the last to surrender.)

The authorities' reaction of execution of the leaders was unwise but perhaps inevitable given the emotional heightening caused by the war in Europe. Even more ominous was the imposition of martial law by General Maxwell. More people were arrested than had taken part in the rising. The country, unusually prosperous because of the war economy, was shaken out of the state of political torpor that had been caused by the postponement of Home Rule. When the rebels had been marched away they had to run a gauntlet of jeering Dubliners who had spent Easter week looting from the damaged stores. (Connolly had been wrong in his copybook Marxist maxim that the British navy would never destroy 'capitalist' property.) Yet by the first weeks of May, when fifteen of the leaders had been shot in what seemed like a sequence deliberately paced for maximum effect, and Casement, awaiting trial in Pentonville, was having the details of his homosexual diaries revealed by the attorney-general, F. E. Smith, the mood of city and country had in Yeats's phrase 'changed utterly'; a terrible beauty – or something – had been born. Yeats's declaration of proprietory interest took the form of a number of poems specifically about the rising, notably the famous 'Easter 1916' quoted above, and many references thereafter, especially the lines about *Cathleen Ni Houlihan* in 'Man and the Echo' written in the year of his death:

> I lie awake night after night
> And never get the answers right.
> Did that play of mine send out
> Certain men the English shot?

The events of the week and the complications of the months before have been the object of intense research and have, or until recently had, passed out of history into hagiography. The idea of a blood sacrifice as necessary irrigation for Ireland's dehydrated cause (with an unstated implication that death forgives killing), formulated then, has been used since to excuse atrocity. 1916 was a copybook Fenian rising with the phoenix already soaring from her own ashes. (Fire and light had always been part of the IRB's liturgy. It was a significant indication of the trend in the Gaelic League that its first newspaper, founded in 1898, was called *Fáinne an Lae* ('Dawn') and that it became *An Claidheamh Soluis*

('The Sword of Light') on 4 August 1900. Coincidentally, a contemporary version of Ingram's 'The Memory of the Dead', written anonymously by a nun, began:

> Who fears to speak of Easter Week?
> Who does its fate deplore?
> The red-gold flame of Ireland's name
> Confronts the world once more.

Many, while understanding the motivation for the rising, were disappointed by it. Reaction among the many Irishmen serving in no-man's-land was deeply divided. 1916 might have had the same effect as Smith O'Brien's skirmish in Widow McCormack's garden or the Fenians' capture of Ballyhurst fort in 1867, but unbelievable bungling by Asquith's government and an obduracy unusual even in the British army produced the effect that Pearse and the others prayed for. The same blimpishness had been displayed by the army from 1915 on at the Western Front when battle fatigue and shellshock were treated with impatience or disdain, and too many soldiers were shot for 'cowardice'. The attitude was epitomised by General Maxwell's vain boast to Lord Wimborne, the lord lieutenant, 'I am going to ensure that there will be no treason whispered for a hundred years.'

Eventually Asquith listened to the resigned chief-secretary's 'birrelling' – a word invented at the time to describe his inimitable gentle and allusive style of speaking words of sound good sense. None of the remaining seventy-four insurgents who had been condemned to death at the courts martial was executed and most of the 1,800 who were interned had been released by the end of 1917. Thomas Ashe (1885–1917) who had successfully staged an ambush on the RIC at Ashbourne in Easter Week, died of pneumonia which followed on bungled force feeding during his hunger-strike in Mountjoy gaol on 25 September 1917. His funeral five days later was the occasion of a huge nationalist demonstration. Michael Collins (1890-1922), who had been a civil servant in London and had served in the GPO, had become the leader of the internees in Frongoch, the detention centre in Wales. He very quickly sensed the altered mood of the country, even if he paid little attention to the noises emanating from the north-east. He set up a superb system of intelligence and prepared for the guerrilla war that he saw as inevitable and necessary.

His more constitutionally inclined partner was Eamon de Valera (1882–1975), the most reluctant leader in Easter Week. His escape from Lincoln gaol on 3 February 1919 had been masterminded by Collins but they were in many senses rivals. It was largely due to de Valera that the Irish Volunteers were subsumed under the borrowed, if not hijacked, cover title, Sinn Féin. This would later take under its wing the reorganised IRB, though with no great enthusiasm by de Valera, who felt that the time for secret societies was past and was opposed to Collins's plans for another insurrection, however effective. Significantly, in Sean O'Casey's 1916 play *The Plough and the Stars* (O'Casey was the historian of Connolly's ICA but like many members was unaware of the plans for the rising) Corporal Stoddart refers to all Dubliners as 'Shinners'. It was technically anachronistic but effectively true by the time of the postwar general election when the composite grouping Sinn Féin (much changed from Griffith's original blueprint and far from having his total approval) won seventy-three of the 105 Irish seats. The old Irish party was left with only six members, though Joe Devlin (1871–1934), the Belfast head of the resurrected Ancient Order of Hibernians (AOH), defeated de Valera in the Falls. De Valera was, however, returned unopposed in Clare.

In Ulster Lloyd George's Government of Ireland Bill (passed 20 December 1920), the granting of devolved parliaments in Belfast and Dublin made partition a reality. The original Lords' amendment had permitted up to nine counties to opt out of Redmond's bill and the historical Ulster would have seemed to be a workable statelet. The Unionists were determined on a 'Protestant parliament for a Protestant people' *aut nihil*. They had unshakable majorities in the four north-eastern counties and they tossed in Derry City and Tyrone and Fermanagh to make 'Northern Ireland' a reasonable social and economic entity. They feared the declining Protestant populations in Donegal, Cavan and Monaghan and excluded them, thereby 'betraying' kith and kin, especially in Donegal. Joe Devlin and other Catholic leaders accepted moral exile for their people rather than risk a bloody and protracted civil war.

As always at the induced birth of a new state the labour pains are pathologically severe and there is no joy after travail. Besides, heightened political activity of any kind had meant, from as early as 1829, sectarian strife on Ulster streets and nocturnal arson in the country. Derry was strongly Sinn Féin and at one with the general mood of the 'Twenty-Six Counties'. In April 1920, the movement of republican prisoners to the city gaol in Bishop Street, between the Catholic Bogside and the Protestant Fountain, sparked riots which lasted until August. The IRA (the Fenian coinage which the new IRB and the Volunteers had adopted) were outgunned by the RIC, now heavily infiltrated by a revived UVF. Fifty people died in the 'Riots', as the prolonged confrontation was called, and when it was ended by army threats of extreme measures visited on both sides it began a period of virtually unbroken quiet in Derry. (This lasted until the famous trouble with the RUC on 5 September 1968 which effectively began the Civil Rights agitation.) The local IRA quickly lost support, and anti-partitionism passed into the watchful hands of the Catholic clergy.

The UVF was given formal recognition with the formation on 1 November 1920 of special constabularies, the most dangerous of which were the 'B'-specials, which remained a virulently anti-Catholic force and were implicated in murder charges as late as August 1969. Sporadic violence continued in Lisburn, Banbridge and Dromore but Belfast, as ever, witnessed the most serious attacks on Catholic property. There was some Catholic retaliation but it was weak, since Catholics were greatly outnumbered and seriously underarmed. 232 people died in 1922 and three million pounds' worth of mainly Catholic working-class property was destroyed. In one notorious case, Owen McMahon, a nationalist politician, and four of his family were killed on

29 March 1922 by men in uniform confidently believed to be 'B'-specials. Eventually peace of a sort was imposed in a kind of quasi-martial law by Dawson Bates, the doctrinaire anti-Catholic Minister of Home Affairs.

In Dublin the results of the 1918 general election led to the setting up of the independent parliament, Dáil Éireann, on 21 January 1919. Since most of the elected members, including de Valera, were still in prison, the impact was muted at first but it was the kind of alternative assembly the dread of which had persuaded Wellington and Peel to grant emancipation at all costs in 1829. The remaining prisoners were released during the first week of March. The tactic proposed by de Valera was to make the force of postwar world opinion grant freedom to the 'small nation' nearest to Britain. He sent Seán T. Ó Ceallaigh as accredited envoy to the Paris peace conference which was called after the Great War. The British delegation's insistence (with the conference's acquiescence) that Ireland was a domestic issue was a blow to de Valera's hopes and increased the intensity of Collins's preparations for war. The divergence between the essentially constitutional Dáil and the IRA widened. In June, de Valera went to America to raise funds and try to persuade the US government to bring moral pressure on Britain. He stayed eighteen months, leaving the field clear for Collins to refine the operation of his intelligence teams and to set up his 'Squad', a crack undercover killing team. The pistol that had been cocked in 1916 was now about to have its trigger pulled. All was ready for a guerrilla war, with the RIC and the British army as the main targets. As in the much more bloody and bitter civil war that followed, a lot of the action was spasmodic, organised by local leaders and with only minimal central control.

By September 1919 a state of insurrection existed, the IRA using localised 'flying columns' as their main means of attack. The government, now led by Lloyd George, responded with flinty heavy-handedness. In 1920 RIC numbers were increased by the notorious 'Black and Tans' (their pied uniforms an indication of the urgency of their deployment). They were mainly ex-servicemen, often officers, and they seemed to overbid the IRA's actions, matching ambushes and burned barracks with reprisals on innocent people and their property. The setting up in July 1920 of the 'Auxies' – the Auxiliary Division of the RIC – identifiable by their glengarry caps and golden harp badges made things much worse. Their behaviour was such that world opinion turned quickly against Britain. There were many individual incidents in the year and a half of the fighting that were to be remembered as part of a noble 'war of independence' and each county later rehearsed 'its fighting story'. Sean Treacy, who is credited with the first action at Soloheadbeg, County Tipperary in January 1919, was killed after a battle with soldiers and G-men (the intelligence arm of the DMP) in Talbot Street, Dublin on 14 October 1920. Thomas MacCurtain, the IRA lord mayor of Cork, was shot in his bed on 19 March 1920, a deed the city coroner found was 'organised and carried out by the Royal Constabulary'. His mayoral place was taken by Terence MacSwiney, who died in Brixton Gaol after a hunger-strike of seventy-four days on 24

October. On the Saturday night of 21 November twelve British officers who had been engaged in intelligence work were eliminated by the 'Squad' in Dublin. The following day at the All-Ireland final Auxies and 'Tans turned their guns on the crowd, killing twelve and injuring sixty. A week later Tom Barry's Cork flying column killed seventeen Auxies at Kilmichael near Macroom. And so it continued, the ferocity of the reprisals increasing with each IRA attack.

Eventually after months of killings, reprisals, burnings and a countrywide climate of fear, Lloyd George gave in to international pressure and general moral affront at home. He wrote to de Valera asking him to attend a peace conference with the new Unionist leader, Sir James Craig. De Valera obtained the approval of Collins and the other leaders of an exhausted IRA and a truce came into effect on 11 July 1921. After three months of preliminary negotiation, a delegation led by Griffith and Collins travelled to London for the Treaty negotiations. De Valera stayed behind, for reasons which are still the subject of debate and conflict.

Of the many nightmares of Irish history, of the kind that Stephen Dedalus was trying to wake from, the 'Treaty' proved the most deadly in the short term and the most vexatious in its persistence in Irish life and politics. The 'Welsh Wizard' was characteristically minatory, threatening on 5 December, 'If I send this letter it will mean war, and war within three days,' and promising that the Twenty-Six Counties would be run as a Crown colony under martial law. He was also duplicitous in that he reassured Craig that the border would stay and that the proposed Boundary Commission would recommend no significant change. Yet the Irish delegates did very well. They obtained significant controls over policing, tariffs and defence but had to accept a partitioned Ireland and a Free State 'faithful to HM King George V'. The draft was signed at 3 o'clock on the morning of 6 December 1921, the remaining plenipotentaries writing their names below that of Griffith, who had signed before Lloyd George's threat. To Collins it was 'freedom to achieve freedom' and to Griffith, it had 'no more finality than that we are the final generation on the face of the earth'. It did not please the IRA, whose sense of betrayal was deep, and it left de Valera in a situation of extreme difficulty. He felt he had to repudiate it because he knew that he would lose whatever control of the militants he still possessed and because he more than any of the delegates knew the importance of the Unionist victory. The cosy and general assumption that the Six Counties could not survive and would eventually sue for unification showed a dire lack of real political acumen. It reckoned nothing on the temperament of the Protestants, who were in permanent exaltation on the metaphorical Walls of Derry, or on the successive British governments that would pay and keep on paying subventions to bolster up the mutilated province rather than admit that it had made yet another mistake about its oldest 'question'. The real miracle was the survival of what by the terms of the Treaty could now officially be called Saorstát Éireann.

Collins returned in muted triumph to a largely relieved Ireland but as he wrote in a letter on the day of the signing:

Think what I have got for Ireland! Something which she has wanted these past seven hundred years. Will anyone be satisfied with the bargain?...I tell you this – early this morning I signed my death warrant. I thought at the time how odd, how ridiculous – a bullet may just as well have done the job five years ago.

14

Saorstát Éireann

There was no absolute reason why the Treaty should have led to civil war except that there was no central authority to prevent it. When it came, it was truly a brothers' war since old comrades found themselves on opposite sides, and even families were divided. After a decade of frenetic activity, of exaltation and disappointment, the country was in a state akin to fugue. Flights from reality abounded and after a world war in which ten million had died and twice that number were seriously wounded, life was held cheap. One cause of violence was the comparative youth of the fighting men and their leaders; another the presence of lately stood-down forces which it would be an exaggeration to call private armies but which were most likely to obey local charismatic leaders. The fight, too, had been for an independent republic, free from any British connection, however formal. It was as hard to turn members of flying columns into politicians as to expect diehard republicans to swear allegiance to a British sovereign, and the situation was vitiated early on when the new state lost two of its leaders with the deaths of Griffith from cerebral haemorrhage on 12 August 1922 and of

Collins in an ambush in County Cork ten days later.

Dáil Éireann had approved the Treaty by sixty-four votes to fifty-seven on 7 January 1922 and almost immediately de Valera resigned the presidency, to be replaced by Griffith. Collins, as chairman of the provisional government, went ahead with the business of accepting sovereignty, taking formal control of Dublin Castle, disbanding the RIC, observing the evacuation of the British troops and doing what he could to persuade Craig to protect northern Catholics. Recruitment for a new unarmed Civic Guard was begun with Eoin O'Duffy (1892–1944) as its first commander, and a National Army with Richard Mulcahy as its GOC relied on British ex-servicemen to boost its numbers. Most of the IRA and Cumann na mBan repudiated the Treaty and by implication the Free State government. De Valera hoped for a non-violent *rapprochement* between the two sides but he found that his influence over the more hotheaded of the anti-Treatyites was negligible. The most implacable of these were Austin Stack (1880–1929), Cathal Brugha (1874–1922), Liam Mellows (1892–1922), Rory O'Connor (1883–1922) and Liam Lynch (1893–1923), who literally could not understand how their military leader could have compromised and suspected quite wrongly that Collins and the rest had been somehow tricked by the enemy. A general election held on 16 June resulted in fifty-eight Treaty members, thirty-six anti-Treaty, and thirty-four miscellaneous. Two days later, when an IRA convention split on the question of a renewed anti-British offensive, the defeated faction, led by O'Connor and Mellows, occupied the Four Courts on Inns

Quay in Dublin. It was essentially a declaration of war. The National Army responded with British artillery, and the badly damaged buildings were evacuated on 30 June. The Public Records Office with its irreplaceable documents was destroyed by the retreating force. Brugha (like Pearse the son of an English father, his name a gaelicisation of the English Burgess) was shot in a melodramatic attempt at a street fight.

The next ten months saw bloodshed more extensive and more damaging than anything in what had begun to be called the 'Tan' war. Seventy-seven IRA men were shot by National Army firing squads and many others killed 'while trying to escape'. On 8 December, O'Connor, Mellows and two others of the Four Courts garrison who had been in custody since June, were shot in retaliation for the IRA killing of Brigadier Sean Hales of the National Army. By the time Saorstát Éireann came into official existence, however, on 6 December 1922 it was clear that the government forces would prevail. De Valera had been tireless in his efforts in bringing about an end to the killing and publicly disavowed any responsibility, personal or on the part of the other anti-Treaty politicians, for the starting or the pursuance of the war. Liam Lynch, who had become chief-of-staff of the IRA when de Valera resigned in June 1922, was killed on 10 April 1923, and on the twenty-seventh of that month de Valera and Frank Aiken (1898–1983), who had replaced Lynch and was later to be a founder of Fianna Fáil, made a unilateral declaration of the end of hostilities. The government did not respond and indeed two IRA men were shot on 2 May. It had by now widespread support and began a mass detention of known or suspected IRA men. There were over 11,000 in prisons or camps by October. A mass hunger strike and two resulting deaths led to further animosity between those who held out and those who gave up or refused to join.

The bitterness in the country was intense and the prospect of a recurrence of anarchy could not be ruled out. The 'Tan' war had elements of nobility about it and played for a world audience; this was a fight to see who would run the country. The granitic relentlessness of the National Army and the government, led by William Cosgrave (1880–1965) and his resolute Minister for Justice, Kevin O'Higgins, may partly be explained by the grief and desolation after Collins's death. It was a classical struggle between pragmatists and dreamers. The terrible beauty had been replaced by hearts fed on fantasies, grown brutal with the fare. Terrible things were done, some to settle old scores and some the result of a generalised desensitisation. The country still has not shaken off the trauma of the Civil War, but it has begun to see it as a necessary if terrible rite of passage to mature statehood.

The country, or the larger part of it that had achieved 'dominion' status, settled down to a kind of normality. Cosgrave proved to be an effective leader although he was unable to move Craig in his determination to yield 'not an inch' and eventually accepted the 1921 border after the report of the 1924 Boundary Commission. Northern Catholics could not help feeling abandoned and all representations to Westminster were shrugged aside as 'a matter for the authorities in Northern Ireland'. Dawson Bates's Offences against the State Act (1924) gave the RUC (founded in 1920) remarkable powers of search, arrest and detention. It was superseded by the even more draconian Special Powers Act in 1932, stated to be the envy of the white supremacist government in South Africa, which was not rescinded until 1972. A few initiatives by individual English ministers and civil servants, seconded to Belfast to establish its bureaucratic systems, to blunt the full confessional nature of the statelet came to nothing. Craig, by now in indifferent health and not much disposed to stand up to his right wing, had insisted that one-third of posts be reserved for Catholics in the civil service as in the RUC. In the police force only a sixth of the assigned places were taken up and here, as in all government services, promotion of Catholics to higher ranks was blocked.

The career prospects for local government employees depended on the political weighting of the council. Newry's and Downpatrick's nationalist majorities meant a reasonable number of jobs for Catholics, while Ballymena and Coleraine showed an appropriately different pattern. One notorious case was Derry City (that nationalists obstinately refused to call Londonderry) where under the proportional represent-ational system guaranteed by Lloyd George's act a Catholic mayor was elected in 1920. Bates's response was to discontinue PR for local elections in 1922 and the city had Unionist mayors until 1968, when the Civil Rights agitation led to the replacement of the city corporation by a development commission. The large Catholic majority was kept in a minority voting situation by ingenious ward boundary manipulation. The counties west of the Bann, the river that acts as a natural north-south demarcation through Ulster, were not as secure as Down, Armagh and Antrim, and when, after the Second World War, multinational companies sought to set up plant, they were steered east. The Protestants who lived to the west understood the need for this economic starvation and, being preferred for most jobs anyway, accepted the situation.

In the 'State' as Ulster people had already begun to call it, the euphoria was replaced by inevitable deflation. (The jigsaw cut border led to inevitable jokes: nationalist travellers to Donegal were, too often, heard to remark 'I'm going north geographically but south politically.') All 'successful' revolutions, even Irish ones, have certain necessary patterns: an element of terror, a bundling together of disparate elements into a military and political alliance which begins to fragment as soon as its short-term goals are achieved and leads to some kind of civil 'war', and the need to derevolutionise the revolutionaries. Traces of the old oppressive regimes are removed and icons are replaced. Memorials to dead heroes are erected and street names are changed, even if older people find it hard to remember them. Armies are reduced to peacetime levels and guerrilla fighters have to face quotidian cares again.

All these elements faced Cumann na nGaedhael (Association of Irishmen), as the pro-Treaty party under Cosgrave called itself from 1923. It successfully weathered the 'army mutiny' of 1924 when the rump of Collins's IRA was dismissed as part of a necessary reduction of establishment from 60,000 to 35,000, and suffered the assassination on 10 July 1927 of Kevin O'Higgins, the deputy leader and chief talent of the party. Quixotically it was Cosgrave's rival, de Valera, now the undisputed leader of the constitutional party which had sloughed off the name Sinn Féin and reconstituted itself as Fianna Fáil ('soldiers of destiny') on 16 May 1926, who played the largest part in 'normalisation'. In a nice piece of semantic juggling, forty-four Fianna Fáil members returned at the general election on 9 June 1927, including 'Dev', found themselves able to disregard the oath as 'an empty political formula', utter with whole consciences the necessary form and take their seats.

The party which their economics expert Sean Lemass (1899–1971) was able to describe as 'slightly constitutional' proved more compact, more vigorous and, allowing for innate Irish conservatism, more amenable to change. It was to be in power from 1932 till 1989, usually with an overall majority, except for fairly brief periods in opposition, 1948–51, 1954–7, 1973–7, 1981–2, 1982–7. When necessary, de Valera, who steadily gained international respect as a statesman, especially as president of the council of the League of Nations in the 1930s, could be as adamantine as any Treatyite in his handling of the IRA. The organisation was declared illegal in June 1936 and again on 9 September 1939, when many members were arrested. During the war, when there were over a thousand interned or imprisoned, nine were executed, three died on hunger strike and six were shot in encounters with armed members of the detective force.

The moral altitude de Valera had achieved by the time of the founding of Fianna Fáil reassured the Catholic Church, which was perceived to have assumed a quasi-executive role in the new state, the bishops' canonical care for faith and morals being interpreted rather broadly. A strict censorship of films was set up in 1923 and the Censorship of Publications Act passed on 16 July 1929 became notorious. As Francis MacManus, one of the few significant contemporary Irish writers not to be proscribed, put it in a radio talk (published in The Years of the Great Test) '... the censorship board ... could ban with a savagery that seemed pathological.' An Appeals Board, established in 1946, had little effect, and there was little change until the amendment act of 1967 'unbanned' 5,000 titles. The board still exists but the virulent puritanism of its early years has gone. Theatre was not censored but in the prevailing climate of suspicion of the artist it was not necessary. Soon the Catholic laity were engaging in self-censorship and the Church was able truthfully to say that they had put no pressure on.

The Catholic Church, though it never was an established religion, was to have its 'special position' recognised by Article 44 of de Valera's 1937 constitution which set up the independent state of 'Éire'. It also contained the Church-influenced Article 41 which enacted that 'no law shall be enacted providing for the grant of a dissolution of marriage'. As in the Six Counties secondary education was confessional.

(The northern bishops had totally rejected Lord Londonderry's well-intentioned attempt to establish non-denominational schools in 1923. They were joined in their opposition by Protestant church leaders.) Both north and south, Catholic secondary schools were run either by religious orders or as diocesan seminaries. Primary schools were under the control of parish priests and many were noted for the disdainful treatment of their teachers, forgetting that *their* vocation was not an entirely religious one, and the poor quality of the school buildings and amenities. Change of attitude was agonisingly slow and since poverty, especially in the intractable west, was as bad as it had been before the foundation of the state, mass education beyond the three Rs, religion and Irish was not a top priority.

Because of the influence of the Gaelic League all of the concomitant parties in the national struggle were committed to the restoration of Irish as the official state language. British stamps with the head of George V were overstamped Saorstát Éireann and plans for a new coinage were set in motion. De Valera's folksy, patriarchal, Gaelic-speaking Ireland with comely maidens, athletic youths and serene firesides was not achievable. Cosgrave was determined to prove his commitment early. On 1 June 1924 new certificate examinations were set up and it was declared that Irish would be a compulsory subject for the Intermediate from 1928 and for the Leaving from 1934. This regulation was in force till 1973, the similar civil service regulation lapsing in 1974. One result was increased investment in the Gaeltacht areas, partly as reward for their long-preserved linguistic virginity and partly to dam emigration from the areas where Irish was the first language.

Even in the matter of Irish, a narrow and mean-minded (and largely puritanical) clique nearly wrecked the worthy endeavour by its unctuous elitism. These were excoriated by the polyonymous Flann O'Brien in his hilarious squib *An Béal Bocht* (1941), at a time when such satire was much needed. The campaign to restore the use of Irish as a spoken language cannot be said to have been successful. The 1995 examination results in the subject showed a pretty dismal performance, though the increase in numbers of government-funded Irish-speaking primary schools and the establishment of a few all-Irish secondary schools in the Six Counties are compensatingly cheering. Many reasonable people have, however, come to cherish Irish for its own sake, to recognise its latent illumination of the Irish psyche and to find a working bilingualism a pleasure and often a convenience.

In spite of anticlimax and disappointment, a majority of the population of the Free State were content enough with the situation and, though euphoria is too strong a word, there was a national satisfaction when Tailteann Games (a kind of revenant Celtic Olympics) were held for the first time in 800 years in August 1924. The Eucharistic Congress in June 1932 drew crowds to Dublin in numbers which had not been seen since Terence Bellew McManus's funeral and would not be seen again till the visit of Pope John Paul II in 1979. There were, too, imaginative schemes for making use of Ireland's few natural resources, notably the promotion of sugar beet harvesting, the establishment of the Electricity

Supply Board to manage the great Shannon hydro-electric scheme and the setting up of the Agricultural Credit Corporation. These were exceptional, however. Agricultural improvements were not exactly unknown but in general older patterns persisted. Ironically it was a new government that gained whatever kudos arose from these improvements. Fianna Fáil got its first overall majority (of one) in the general election of 1933. No longer dependent on Labour, de Valera felt himself able to shrug off the IRA well-wishers who had 'protected' his candidates so fiercely during the election. Another band of hustings 'protectors', O'Duffy's Army Comrades Association, had joined with Cumann na nGaedheal to form the Fine Gael (roughly='Irish tribe') party.

One of de Valera's first acts, a fortnight after forming his government, was to remove O'Duffy from his post as commissioner of the Garda Síochána. His association began calling itself the National Guard and assumed Fascist lineaments, becoming 'Blueshirts' in fraternal tribute to Hitler's Brown- and Mussolini's Blackshirts. The next two years were marked by low-level but fundamentally serious clashes between Blueshirts and the IRA. Legislation against the wearing of uniforms (21 March 1934) and the proscribing of the association led to a rapidly changing sequence of names. The wiser members of Fine Gael soon dissociated themselves from all forms of O'Duffyism and reverted like their rivals to parliamentary procedures, but the label 'Blueshirt' lingered for many years. The main plank of their political platform, support of the farmers during the bitter 'economic war' that followed de Valera's refusal to pay Britain land annuities, largely lost its force when the 'coal-cattle' pact of 1935 mitigated the worst severities of the depression that resulted. The 'war' ended with an Irish payment of £10 million (against a British claim of £104 million) and the handing over of the Treaty Ports to Ireland in 1936.

The 1937 Constitution Amendment Bill removed the King and the Governor-General and called the Free State 'Éire', proving rather sadly that Collins's views about the Treaty (partition excepted) were correct. The general election and constitution referendum of July of that year showed a majority of 13 per cent in favour of the change and a rather nerve-wracking tied result in seats. This was rectified in June 1938, when Fianna Fáil's majority was sixteen. The party was to stay in power for a ten year span which included the Second World War. Political coloration was still largely determined by the Treaty but de Valera commanded great support. Even the embattled farmers were stoical during his fiscal battle with Britain, and many were nominal shareholders in his newspaper, the *Irish Press*, which he founded in 1931.

De Valera's finest hour was his tightrope walk of what may be called with a little forcing his covertly pro-British neutrality during the war. German invasion was always a possibility and there was no attempt either at blocking the enlistment of 50,000 Irish nationals in the British forces or at approval of conscription in the north. As in the Great War, many Irish men and women joined up because of the employment opportunities offered and 93,000 risked conscription by emigrating to England. That was one serious social evil that Fianna Fáil were not able to cure. Infiltration by German spies was considerably less than the heated copywriters of Fleet Street claimed, and captured British servicemen, unlike their enemies, were repatriated. Like most Irishmen, de Valera was aware of the evils of Nazism but the continuing partition of Ireland made a mockery in nationalist eyes of fighting for democratic freedom and a country's right to self-determination. Overt (and instinctive) punctiliousness led him to risk great criticism on 2 May 1945 when he visited the German Embassy to offer condolences on the death of Hitler. His action horrified the small Jewish community in Ireland.

Postwar Ireland was hit by strikes of farm labourers, industrial workers and primary teachers. This last was a protracted and bitter affair and persisted from 20 March to 30 October 1946. The mediator was Archbishop McQuaid, whose thirty-two year incumbency from 1940 was marked by public crozier-wielding and secret care for the poor. He led the opposition to the Mother and Child scheme of the Health minister, Dr Noel Browne, who had all but eradicated tuberculosis, and effectively brought down the Coalition government in 1951. The reaction of later generations to the affair was one of incredulity, and has led to a persistent questioning of what exactly is the teaching of the Church in social matters.

The 1948 general election returns gave Fianna Fáil sixty-eight seats, eleven less than the combined total of the opposition. John A. Costello (1891–1976), a leading barrister and TD for Dublin South-East, became Taoiseach of a remarkably variegated coalition government. Its Minister for External Affairs was Seán MacBride, the son of Maud Gonne and of John MacBride who was executed after Easter Week. He had founded a left-wing party called Clann na Poblachta ('Children of the Republic') in 1946, and it was mainly at his urging that Costello declared, rather precipitately, on 21 December 1948, that Éire was a republic. It did not do much good to the cause of anti-partition but then nothing did. MacBride refused to let the new republic join NATO because of 'Britain's claim to sovereignty in Northern Ireland'. The coalition collapsed when, unaccountably, MacBride joined the right wing and refused to proceed with Noel Browne's health scheme. After the general election in May 1951, Fianna Fáil were returned with a majority of seventy-four to sixty-nine, but dependent on the votes of the independent candidates.

In an article written in 1949 for the Jesuit magazine, *The Month* Seán O'Faolain described what he had already dubbed the 'Grocers' Republic' as the place where 'a policeman's lot is a supremely happy one. God smiles, the priest beams, and the novelist groans.' He had brightened a period that he called, 'pretty damn dull' by his editorship of *The Bell* from 1941 to 1946. This monthly magazine had been founded by Peadar O'Donnell, republican labour activist and novelist, and was to continue under his editorship until 1954. It showed Ireland its own face and persuaded the country that it had a head as well as a soul. It found writers who became famous and caused the controversy that its editors thought was the primary role of the artist. O'Faolain took on Dr Michael Browne, the Bishop of Galway, regarded as being Dev's spiritual director, in a famous letter in September 1951, telling him that he could not have the 'abject compliance' that he sought. In his final editorial, written in April 1946 he expressed his weariness at having to abuse 'our bourgeoisie, pietists, Tartuffes, Anglophobes, Celtophiles, et *alli hujus generis.*'

The next fifty years were to see a revolution in Ireland more fundamental than anything in its history. The nature of Church–state relations was considerably modified, and doubts have continued to be expressed about the Church's right to influence legislation for what many see as a pluralist society. To take two examples, the prohibition on the importation of contraceptives first imposed in 1935 was removed in 1973 and by 1993 they were on unlimited sale. In 1986, a referendum to allow divorce was defeated, but towards the end of 1995, a new proposal to end de Valera's constitutional ban on remarriage was carried by the narrowest of majorities.

The social change was hastened by a small economic miracle wrought by Seán Lemass's postwar economic policies (prescribed by T. K. Whitaker, the head of the civil service), by the renewal in the Church generated by Pope John XXIII, by the coming of a national television network, RTE, in 1961 and by Ireland's joining the EEC (later EU) in 1973. Old certainties were shaken and old pieties reassessed. Ireland was part of the global village and even her rural fastnesses were affected by world trends. She had joined the

United Nations in 1955 and her soldiers were to serve with distinction in Cyprus, Lebanon, the Congo and the Balkans. Her young people were as aware of the Swinging Sixties as any Carnaby Street Quantifier and responded in a tempered way to student protest. The social and psychological high point of the 1960s was the visit by US President John F. Kennedy in the summer before his assassination, his tour studiously avoiding the Six Counties. His shocking death on 22 November 1963 caused him to join for a while, as icon, John XXIII and Patrick Pearse. More cynical observers might opt for the first broadcast of Gay Byrne's *Late Late Show* on 6 July 1962 as the most significant event of the decade, and the fall-out from Lemass's visit to Terence O'Neill (1914–90) on 14 January 1965 has still to be fully assessed.

15

Dreary Spires

It is impossible for any historian to pronounce upon what have been called the 'troubles' in the north of Ireland. Causes are frequently asserted with different degrees of rhetoric; more perverse commentators are likely to find themselves logically back at Baginbun. After partition the province survived, mostly peaceful, propped up by Westminster. There was occasional rioting, sometimes quite vicious, as in July 1935 when, after an Orange parade, there were nine days of violence with nine deaths and 514 Catholics driven from their homes in the York Street area of Belfast.

One principle that Craig (Lord Craigavon since 1927) had insisted upon – and he was a doughty insister – was parity of provision with Britain. All citizens benefited from the Attlee government's welfare state. The NHS, family allowances and, with the 1947 Education Act, free secondary education with the option of appropriate third-level for those who were capable of it, did much to improve the quality of Catholic life. Though still second choices and barred from any significant promotion in the public service, Catholics did not feel the same absolute need to emigrate as once they had done. Middle class Catholics (businessmen, lawyers, doctors, teachers, with mainly Catholic clients, and imperial civil servants who had managed home postings), especially those who lived in the east, were likely to have some Protestant friends. The impatient Catholic young, now well educated, vowed themselves tired of old quarrels and tended to mock the Nationalist MPs and councillors who had gone to the unimaginable lengths – for a party whose instincts were abstentionist – of becoming Her Majesty's loyal opposition in 1965.

The political stasis of the gerontocracy in Stormont, the ridiculously grand parliament buildings that were opened on 16 November 1932, was broken when Terence O'Neill became prime minister in 1963. O'Neill succeeded the sectarian grandee Lord Brookeborough, whose twenty-year period of office was undistinguished, except by apparent lack of awareness of the existence of Catholics and a tendency to idleness. O'Neill's able Minister of Home Affairs, Brian Faulkner (1921–77), defeated 'Operation Harvester', the IRA's campaign of the years 1956–62, mainly because it had little support from northern Catholics. (His attempt, in 1971, to stop IRA insurgence by the internment that had worked so well before blew up in his face.) The meeting between Lemass and O'Neill in 1965 was low-key and stated to be about closer economic ties. It was followed by others and when Jack Lynch became Taoiseach in 1966, he too made the journey north.

Grassroots Protestant reaction was swift and antique. As so often in the past, the voice of adamant Protestantism was loud and clear and it was incorporated in the Rev Ian Paisley. He was a brilliant, tireless and immensely strong orator, anti-Catholic and anti-papal. He scented change with the coming of O'Neill and he was also aware of the prime minister's weakness and superficiality. Paisley's appearance on the election platform of James Kilfedder in West Belfast in 1964 was followed by 1930-style riots in Divis Street and he had soon gathered enough of a following to form the Democratic Unionist Party (DUP) in 1971. Before that he had set himself up as O'Neill's particular gadfly, finally helping to drive him out of politics. He was at once the vocal manifestation of suspicious Protestantism and its manipulator. He exposed the weakness of the polite moves of reconciliation and his province-wide support was much greater than it appeared.

More ominous than Paisleyism was the spectre of militant Protestantism that was already haunting the scene with the resurgence of the UVF, which claimed responsibility for the deaths of two Catholics in 1966. The foundation of the Northern Ireland Civil Rights Association (NICRA) in January 1967 seemed in keeping with the spirit of the decade as celebrated outside in the real world. Its membership was mainly Catholic but it had student members who would not be labelled. The most keenly felt injustice was in the allocation of council housing, especially in mixed-population towns. The best known example was Derry, where a significant Nationalist majority had been ruled by a Unionist council since the abolition of PR in 1922. The notorious case of a nineteen-year-old unmarried Protestant typist being given a house in Caledon, County Tyrone, where married Catholics with families were clearly more deserving, led to the first action in what was to be called the Civil Rights movement. Austin Currie, the young MP, occupied the house until he was removed by the police. The publicity encouraged other actions and on 3 October 1968 when William Craig, Minister of Home Affairs, banned a NICRA march organised by Eamonn McCann and Eamonn Melaugh of the Derry Housing Action Committee, the scene was set for a confrontation which was to have remarkable consequences.

Nationalists were used to bannings and reroutings but the times they were a-changing. Derry people were sore about imposed economic stagnation, about losing the new university which had been sited at safe Protestant Coleraine by the Lockwood Committee even though Derry's Magee College was an obvious nucleus, and about Unionist 'occupation' of their city. NICRA decided to defy the ban and the march began as scheduled on the following Saturday. The resulting police and 'B'-special violence was seen worldwide on television. The riots (and looting) that followed lasted well into the following Sunday morning. They were the first serious civic disturbances in Derry since the early 1920s but they were to be repeated many times. Harold Wilson's Labour government was shaken into action and within the year the main demands of the marchers had been met: the RUC was to be reformed, the 'B'-specials disbanded, Derry's corporation was replaced by a commission pending a thorough revision of local government, housing allocation was to be administered by an independent body and the 'business' local government vote which had led to the street-cry of 'One man: one vote!' was abolished.

These reforms pleased the mass of NICRA supporters who had nothing more revolutionary in mind, but in January 1969 a six-day march from Belfast to Derry by the radical students' movement People's Democracy, which was attacked by Protestant extremists at Burntollet Bridge near Derry and again in the largely Protestant Waterside area of the city, showed that palliation was not enough. The police and 'B'-specials were almost certainly involved; at best they took no action against the attackers of a legal peaceful march. By the end of April Terence O'Neill had resigned as prime minister, his place being taken by James Chichester-Clarke, his political *doppelganger*, and his leaving hastened by the sabotage by the UVF at the Silent Valley Reservoir, at the time blamed on the IRA. The early summer was uneasy with riots (a regular occurrence especially around the 12 July anniversary of the Boyne) and attacks on Catholic homes and flats in Belfast. Much more serious was the violent and protracted ending of the traditional Apprentice Boys march in Derry on 12 August.

John Hume, leader of the Derry Citizens Action Committee, had tried to have the march banned. After three days of police versus citizenry battles he and other nationalist leaders contributed to persuading the Northern Ireland government to ask its Westminster counterpart for the assistance of the British Army. As if by signal there were Protestant attacks on Catholic homes in West Belfast. The Catholics were virtually defenceless except for a few old IRA guns. Figures published at the end of the month showed that ten people had been killed and, of the 899 injuries reported, 154 had been gunshot wounds. The army took to the streets of Belfast on 16 August and were welcomed as peacemakers. The visit of James Callaghan, then Home Secretary, increased nationalist euphoria which lasted, apart from some routine rioting in Belfast and Derry, until the following June. By this time a regenerated IRA had begun a calculated campaign to finish the business of reunification. The army proved to be a poor police force and the next twenty-four years were to see an armed struggle between the IRA, the more fundamentalist wing calling itself 'provisional' after a conference in 1969, and the security forces which now comprised a slowly changing RUC, the Ulster Defence Regiment (UDR – the name was later chaged to the Royal Irish Regiment) which many nationalists regarded as renamed 'B'-specials, and the army, which had not been able to leave Belfast or Derry or Northern Ireland in general since its mobilisation. Various Protestant groups: UVF, Ulster Defence Association (UDA), Ulster Freedom Fighters (UFF) and others, engaged in a specifically anti-Catholic campaign. Internecine struggles were common among both Loyalist and Republican paramilitary groupings.

Recruitment to the IRA was given a great boost by the hamfisted imposition of a selective and inefficient internment of 342 people, all but a few of them Catholics, on 9 August 1971 and by the events of 'Bloody Sunday' (30 January 1972) in Derry when thirteen unarmed Catholics were shot by soldiers of the First Parachute Regiment during an anti-internment march. Northern Ireland had to get used to murderous riots, destruction by explosives of 'economic' targets, the threat of gun attacks on pubs and even halls of worship. The violence spilled over into the Republic, notably when, during the Ulster Workers' Council (UWC) strike against the 'power-sharing executive' in May 1974, twenty-five people were killed by car-bombs in Dublin, and six in Monaghan. Bombing British cities, though much more dangerous than the 'soft' targets at home, was considered a prime tactic and continued into the 1990s. The hunger strikes of 1980–1 (ostensibly because of the refusal of the authorities to allow prisoners to wear their own clothes) led to the moving and courageous deaths of ten IRA prisoners. By the end of 1990, 2,800 people had been killed and 32,000 seriously injured. The North showed the scars of civil disorder and military occupation (where the queen's writ ran).

The years 1969–1994 saw, on the nationalist side, another kind of struggle between the forces of constitutionalism and paramilitarism, both claiming the same goals, both secure in their moral rectitude. The numbers actively engaged in what opponents and journalists called 'terrorism' was small on both sides, but the great mass of the population believed that their opposite numbers secretly supported the para-militaries on their side. Nationalists were given reason enough to believe that there were cases of collusion between the security forces and the Protestant gangs. The para-militaries, because of their psychological set, were subject only to their own logic and morality. Though, with some horrific exceptions, the situation never reached the intense and savage cruelty of the Middle East or Bosnia, not all the operations nor non-military activities were informed by noble motives. The notion of 'legitimate' targets gave rise to much justifiable criticism, and some accusations of racketeering and gang-warfare are sustainable. The present cessation of violence, which has cheered all Irish citizens, is still felt to be on a knife-edge, partly because of the old problem that faces peacemakers the world over: what to do with a standing army after a war.

In fact, life in Northern Ireland continued more or less 'normally' and people got used to body searches and travel delays. All main roads from the Republic had permanent checkpoints, and minor roads were cratered. There were few who were not touched by the 'troubles' in some way or other and well-rehearsed jokes suggested 'Shop early while shops last' and that the career most likely to lead to permanent employment was glazing.

The main arm of nationalist constitutionalism, the Social Democratic and Labour Party (SDLP), was founded in 1970 with Gerry Fitt (Lord Fitt of Bell's Hill since 1983) as its head. One of its long-term aims was the securing of a united Ireland by consent and it has held to that aim in spite of criticism from the IRA and the Unionist opposition. Its great achievement was its convincing of Westminster of the need for a Dublin involvement in all considerations of Northern Ireland's future. Its leader since 1979 has been John Hume, and to him must go the credit of holding together a fairly wide spectrum grouping and of being a significant player in the brokering of the IRA ceasefire. The party showed its ability when it held office during the brief life of the executive set up after the Sunningdale agreement and in its patient continuance after the UWC strike brought down that executive. The Anglo-Irish Agreement, signed by Prime Minister Margaret Thatcher and Garret FitzGerald (then Taoiseach of the 1982–7 coalition) on 15 August 1985, an agreement which set up a permanent British-Irish intergovernmental conference and to which Ulster said, 'No!' was initiated by its efforts. So was the Downing Street agreement of Albert Reynolds and John Major of 15 December 1993, which disclaimed all British interest of a selfish nature and established the 'right of the Irish people alone, by agreement between the two parts . . . to exercise their right to self-determination'.

Hume argued that with the Downing Street Declaration the reasons for continuing a campaign of violence had been removed, and his meetings with Gerry Adams, President of Sinn Féin, begun in 1988, resulted in a cessation of violence on 30 August 1994. The 'peace process' has not been a rapid one, the sticking points being the refusal of the IRA to decommission their arms before all-party talks. The Unionists have refused to attend any talks until decommissioning has taken place and apparently the DUP has refused to attend any talks with members of Sinn Féin. The Northern Ireland Office are felt by many to favour the Unionist point of view. One of the high-visibility brokers is President Clinton, whose personal visit to Belfast in December 1995 contributed to hopes of a breakthrough. The plain people of Northern

Ireland are relishing the sight of the paraphernalia of 'trouble' – watchtowers, permanent checkpoints, ramps – being dismantled. A tropical summer which brought a large number of tourists in 1995 increased the cheer. The more sanguine believe that such happy welcoming of a kind of normality is the best index of continuing peace.

The Republic has learnt during the twenty-five years of violence to take the northern problem seriously, and to understand its nature perhaps for the first time since the seventeenth century. The unfortunate Arms Affair which led to the sacking of Neil Blaney and Charles J. Haughey, the attack on the British Embassy after the Belfast violence in 1969 and its destruction on 2 February 1972 after 'Bloody Sunday', the 'fund-gathering' raids on southern banks, the need to increase the establishment of garda and army in border counties, the resentment at being called a 'safe haven for terrorists' – all these kept the North on the front pages of Irish newspapers and in Dáil reports. Fianna Fáil's instinctive support for northern nationalists left them open to accusations of being soft on the Provos, while Fine Gael's sometimes unctuous reminders of the rights and fears of Unionists were eventually paid more heed. The 'Irish Dimension', incorporated after Sunningdale, was accepted by all subsequent southern governments and rarely was the 'situation' used to make political capital, this in the most highly politicised country in the EU.

Lemass's 'economic miracle' came a little unstuck with the oil crisis of the mid-1970s but the slump was weathered as well, if not better, than in other western countries. The recession of the 1980s again saw an increase of emigration but it was largely by skilled workers and university graduates from a country with a remarkably high standard of education and small opportunity. The most notable change, accelerated after EEC membership, was an increase in welfare provision and the gradual diminution of the Catholic Church's political and social influence. Ecclesiastical attitudes to censorship, contraception, the right to abortion (or at least information about where it might be obtained), and divorce are not automatically accepted as they had been in the era of de Valera. Recent revelations about erring pastors have made clerical pronouncements less dogmatic. The Church's authority to speak on faith and morals has not been discountenanced but the area covered by those two terms has been redefined. Irish people are still practising Catholics with a regularity and in numbers unique in western Europe and many hope that the Church's present crisis will lead to renewal and greater honesty.

The 'free' part of Ireland is young in age and as aesthetically and culturally self-confident as other members of the EU. The response to the award of a fifth Nobel prize, to the Ulster poet Seamus Heaney, is a demonstration of a strong literary tendency and a pride in the international standing of its writers and dramatists. Its contribution to popular music, film and other literary forms is recognised. On this anniversary of its greatest affliction, the Famine, there is some satisfaction in the changes a hundred and fifty years can make. This artistic reputation may not seem important or desirable to the 'hard cold fire of the Northerner' but the Republic, with its economic buoyancy, its rapidly improving welfare provision, and the general improvement of its amenities (subvented by generous grants from Brussels) appears a more desirable partner than when de Valera's frugal comfort and a stoic disdain for materialism was all it had to offer. The glamour of its reputation was increased when Mary Robinson became president in 1990. She continued the process of erasing Ireland's old reputation as a place of violence, backwardness and unthinking subservience to the Church.

Both Fianna Fáil and Fine Gael have proved to be more centrist than their earlier reputations might have suggested, and Labour has found it possible to work in coalition with each. The parties have always prided themselves on the accessibility of their TDs and though a client system is believed to exist, accusations of corruption are seldom made and harder to prove. Young voters are not susceptible to Treaty rhetoric. Urban crime, often associated with drug abuse, is the seamy side of comparative affluence allied with persistent inequality, but outside the larger towns, crime rates are low by European standards. The state of suspense associated with the bogging down of the peace process is felt more keenly in the North; the South has other business to attend to and it can hope for no short-term advantage from a settlement of whatever kind. Yet it accepts its responsibility of playing its part in bringing light where there was more usually heat and of hoping to find after far too long the answer to the Irish question.

A CHRONOLOGY OF IRISH HISTORY

30000 bc	Ireland's topography established
7000–6500 bc	Human habitation at Mount Sandel
2500 bc	Building of passage graves, notably Newgrange
1200 bc	Late bronze-age artefacts
680 bc	Circular habitation enclosure at Emain Macha
AD 1–500	Building of crannogs, hill forts and raths
77–84	Agricola, Roman governor of Britain, eventually decides against invasion
200	Conn Céd-cathach establishes high kingship of Tara
300–450	Irish raids on Roman Britain
400	Eoghan and Conall, sons of Niall Noígiallach, establish kingdom of Aileach
432	Traditional date of the coming of St Patrick
563	Colum Cille begins his mission to Iona
575	Convention of Druim Cett
597	Death of Colum Cille
664	Synod of Whitby
795	First Viking raids
841	Foundation of permanent Viking colony in Dublin
964	Rise of Dál Cais and beginning of hegemony of Brian Boru
975–1014	Brian king of Munster and later of Ireland
1014	Battle of Clontarf and death of Brian
1132–1148	Reforming activity of St Malachy
1155	Bull *Laudabiliter*
1166	Expulsion of Dermot MacMurrough
1170	Landing of Strongbow
1171	Death of Dermot. Henry II lands in Ireland
1175	John de Courcy invades Ulster
1176	Death of Strongbow
1177	Prince John made lord of Ireland; Cork and Limerick granted to Norman vassals
1210	King John's second visit to Ireland; submission of Irish kings
1224	First Irish Dominican and Franciscan foundations
1315	Edward Bruce lands at Larne
1318	Death of Edward Bruce at Faughart
1348	Black Death kills about one-third of the population
1394–5	Richard II's first expedition. Defeat of Art McMurrough and general submission of all but northern chiefs
1460–8	Supremacy of Desmond, ends with his execution by Worcester
1478-1513	Rule of Garret Mór Fitzgerald
1492	Poynings' Law makes Dublin parliament subservient to that in London

1534	Rebellion of 'Silken Thomas'
1541	Henry VIII proclaimed king of Ireland
1557–8	Establishment of 'King's' and 'Queen's Counties in Offaly and Laois
1561	Rebellion of Shane O'Neill in Ulster (murdered by MacDonnells in 1567)
1587	Hugh O'Neill proclaimed Earl of Tyrone
1588	Ships of Spanish Armada wrecked on Ulster coast
1595–1603	Nine Years War between O'Neill, O'Donnell and English forces
1598	Battle of the Yellow Ford
1601	O'Neill's defeat at Kinsale
1607	'Flight of the Earls'
1608–10	British colonisation of Ulster
1639	'Black Oath' imposed on Ulster Scots by Wentworth
1641	Outbreak of Ulster rebellion
1642	Owen Roe O'Neill takes command of Irish forces
1646	Battle of Benburb
1649	Cromwell arrives in Ireland. Massacres at Drogheda, Wexford. Premature death of Owen Roe
1652	Act for the Settling of Ireland
1653	Forfeiture of Irish lands and transplantation
1679	Arrest of Oliver Plunkett (executed, 1681)
1687	Tyrconnell Lord Deputy
1688	Closing of the gates of Derry
1689	Siege of Derry lifted
1690	Battle of Boyne
1691	Treaty of Limerick
1695	Penal laws
1704	Further penal laws (Queen Anne's reign).
1760	Thurot lands French force at Carrickfergus
1782	Dungannon convention of Volunteers
1791	Foundation of United Irishmen in Belfast
1792–93	Relief acts remove most Catholic disabilities
1795	'Battle of the Diamond' at Loughgall, Co Armagh leads to founding of the Orange Order
1798	Rebellion breaks out in Wexford, Antrim and Down. McCracken and other leaders hanged. Tone, captured in Lough Swilly, commits suicide
1800	Act of Union
1829	Catholic Emancipation
1831–4	Tithe War
1840	Daniel O'Connell founds Repeal Association
1842	Charles Gavan Duffy becomes editor of *Nation*, organ of Young Ireland movement
1843	Repeal mass meeting for Clontarf cancelled
1845–48	Famine caused by potato blight. Population reduced by two million by death and emigration
1845	Queen's Colleges founded in Belfast, Galway and Cork
1847	Death of Daniel O'Connell
1857	Serious sectarian disturbances in Belfast

1858	IRB established in Dublin
1859	Fenian Brotherhood set up in US
1861	Derryveagh evictions
1862	Shipbuilding firm of Harland & Wolff founded
1866	Archbishop Paul Cullen becomes first Irish cardinal
1867	Unsuccessful Fenian rising
1869	Disestablishment of Church of Ireland
1873	Home Rule League founded
1877	J. G. Biggar devises 'obstructive' tactics for Irish Parliamentary party
1880	Parnell head of Irish Parliamentary party
1886	Lord Randolph Churchill's anti-Home Rule visit to Belfast
1893	Gaelic League founded
1900	John Redmond unites Irish party
1905	Formation of Ulster Unionist Council and pro-Home Rule Dungannon Clubs (the latter by Bulmer Hobson)
1908	Foundation of ITGWU and Griffith's Sinn Féin
1910	Carson becomes leader of Irish Unionists
1911	Lords' veto abolished
1912	Solemn League & Covenant
1913	Foundation of Ulster Volunteer Force and Irish Citizens Army
1914	Curragh 'mutiny'; UVF gun-running; Home Rule Bill becomes law but shelved till end of war (from 4 August)
1915	IRB reorganised
1916	Easter rising; Unionists agree to a partitioned Ulster
1919	Action at Soloheadbeg, Co Tipperary, considered first action of 'War of Independence'
1920	Sectarian riots in Belfast and Derry; formation of Ulster Special Constabulary begins; Ulster partitioned under Government of Ireland Act, Sir James Craig prime minister; sporadic violence and ambushes, mobilisation of Irregulars and Auxiliary Division ('Black and Tans' and 'Auxies'); 'Bloody Sunday'
1921	Truce and peace conference; Anglo-Irish treaty
1922	Outbreak of Civil War; death of Arthur Griffith, Michael Collins; Special Powers Act (NI)
1924	Army 'mutiny'
1925	After failure of Boundary Commission existing border accepted
1926	De Valera founds Fianna Fáil
1927	Assassination of Kevin O'Higgins; Fianna Fáil enters Dáil
1932	De Valera new president of Executive Council. Fianna Fáil government; tariff 'war' begun after witholding of land annuities
1933	Blueshirt activity with O'Duffy as leader
1937	New constitution replaces Free State with Éire
1938	Tariff agreement between Britain and Éire
1939	Éire declares neutrality

1940	UK reimposes trade sanctions
1941	Heavy German air-raids in Belfast; damage from German bombs in Dublin, killing thirty people
1948	Declaration of republic by Costello as head of coalition; N Ireland shares benefits of Britain's 'welfare state'
1951	Noel Browne, coalition Health Minister, resigns after clerical opposition to his 'Mother and Child' scheme (de Valera sets up similar scheme in 1953); guarantee by Britain of NI's remaining part of UK at its parliament's discretion
1956–62	Operation Harvest – IRA's border campaign
1963	Terence O'Neill becomes PM of NI
1965	Sean Lemass and O'Neill meet at Stormont. Opposition by Ian Paisley; Nationalist party becomes official opposition at Stomont.
1967	Northern Ireland Civil Rights Asssociation (NICRA) formed
1968	Police clash with NICRA marchers in Derry followed by severe rioting
1969	People's Democracy march attacked at Burntollet; after a spring and summer of rioting and growing tension army called out to keep peace in Derry and (after anti-Catholic disturbances) in Belfast
1970	Start of Provisional IRA's campaign (lasts till 1994); answered by intermittent Protestant terrorist activity; Social Democratic and Labour party (SDLP) founded by moderate nationalists
1971	Continuing IRA campaign leads to internment; Paisley's Democratic Unionist party (DUP) founded
1972	Thirteen anti-interment demonstrators killed in Derry; Stormont prorogued
1973	Sunningdale Agreement leads to formation of power-sharing executive
1974	Executive brought down by UWC general strike
1976	'Peace People' movement
1977	Brian Faulkner, last prime minister of NI, dies in hunting accident
1981	Ten hunger strikers die in 'special category' campaign; severe violence and increase in following of IRA
1985	Anglo-Irish Agreement between Margaret Thatcher and Garret FitzGerald
1987	Remembrance Day bomb in Enniskillen kills eleven people
1988	Talks between Gerry Adams of Sinn Féin and John Hume of SDLP
1986	Referendum confirms constitutional ban on divorce
1993	Downing Street Declaration signed by John Major and Albert Reynolds as a result of many secret talks
1994	IRA ceasefire; Protestant paramilitary ceasefire
1995	Divorce referendum passed by narrow majority in Republic. Visit of US President Bill Clinton

SELECT BIBLIOGRAPHY

Adamnán. *Vita Columbae* (ed. W. Reeves). Dublin, 1857.

Adamson, I. *The Cruthin.* Bangor, 1974.

————. *The Identity of Ulster.* Belfast, 1982.

Akenson, D. H. *The Irish Education Experiment: The National System of Education in the Nineteenth Century.* London, 1970.

Arthur, P. and Jeffery, K. *Northern Ireland Since 1968.* Oxford, 1988.

Bardon, J. *A History of Ulster.* Belfast, 1992.

Barrington, J. *The Rise and Fall of the Irish Nation.* Paris, 1833.

Bartlett, T. and Hayton, D. (eds.) *Penal Era and Golden Age: Essays in Irish History 1690–1800.* Belfast, 1979.

Beckett, J. C. *The Making of Modern Ireland 1603–1923.* London, 1966.

Bew, P. *Conflict and Conciliation in Ireland 1890–1910.* Oxford, 1987.

Blake, J. W. *Northern Ireland in the Second World War.* Belfast, 1956.

Brady, C. and Gillespie, R. *Natives and Newcomers; the Making of Irish Colonial Society 1534–1641.* Dublin, 1986.

Brown, M. *The Politics of Irish Literature.* London, 1971.

Brown, T. *Ireland: A Social and Cultural History.* London, 1981.

Buckland, P. *Irish Unionism* Vol I: *The Anglo-Irish and the New Ireland 1885–1922.* Vol II: *Ulster Unionism and the Origins of Northern Ireland 1886–1922.* Dublin, 1973.

————. *The Factory of Grievances: Devolved Government in Northern Ireland 1921–39.* Dublin, 1979.

Canny, N. *From Reformation to Restoration.* Dublin, 1987.

Chadwick, N. *The Celts.* London, 1970.

Clarke, A. *The Old English in Ireland.* London, 1966.

Clarke, H. B. (ed.). *Irish Cities.* Cork, 1995.

Collins, P. (ed.). *Nationalism and Unionism: Conflict in Ireland 1885–1921.* Belfast, 1994.

Connolly, S. *Priests and People in Pre-Famine Ireland 1780–1845.* Dublin, 1982.

Coogan, T. P. *Ireland since the Rising.* London, 1966.

————. *The IRA.* London, 1980.

————. *The Troubles.* London, 1995.

Corish, P. J. *The Catholic Community in the Seventeenth and Eighteenth Centuries.* Dublin, 1981.

Cosgrove, A. *Late Medieval Ireland.* Dublin, 1981.

Crawford, W. H. and Trainor, B. (eds.). *Aspects of Irish Social History 1750–1800.* Belfast, 1969.

Curtis, E. *A History of Ireland.* London, 1936.

de Paor, L. *Divided Ulster*. London, 1970.

Davitt, M. *The Fall of Feudalism in Ireland*. New York, 1904.

Dickson, R. H. *Ulster Emigration to Colonial America 1718–1785*. Belfast, 1966.

Doherty, J. E. and Hickey, D. J. *A Chronology of Irish History since 1500*. Dublin, 1989.

Doyle, D. N. *Ireland, Irishmen and Revolutionary America 1760–1820*. Dublin, 1981.

Edwards, R. D. and Williams, T. D. *The Great Famine*. London, 1956.

Edwards, R. D. *Patrick Pearse: the Triumph of Failure*. London, 1977.

Elliott, M. *Partners in Revolution: The United Irishmen and France*. London, 1982.

Farrell, M. *Northern Ireland: the Orange State*. London, 1976.

Fisk, R. *In Time of War: Ireland, Ulster and the Price of Neutrality 1939–1945*. London, 1983.

Foster, R. F. *Modern Ireland 1600–1972*. London, 1988.
————. *Paddy and Mr Punch*. London, 1993.
————(ed.). *The Oxford History of Ireland*. Oxford, 1989.

Gray, J. *City in Revolt: James Larkin and the Belfast Dock Strike of 1907*. Belfast, 1985.

Harkness, D. W. *Northern Ireland since 1920*. Dublin, 1983.

Johnston, E. M. *Great Britain and Ireland 1760–1800*. Edinburgh, 1963.

Kennedy, L. and Ollerenshaw, P. (eds.). *An Economic History of Ulster 1820–1940*. Manchester, 1985.

Kearney, H. C. *The British Isles*. Cambridge, 1989

Kee, R. *The Green Flag*. London, 1970.

Kinealy, C. *This Great Calamity: Irish Famine, 1845–52*. Dublin, 1994.

Lacy, B., *Siege City, The Story of Derry and Londonderry*. Belfast, 1990.

Lee, J. *Ireland 1912–1985, Politics and Society*. Cambridge, 1989.
————.*The Modernisation of Irish Society 1848–1918*. Dublin, 1973.

Litton, H. *Irish Famine: an Illustrated History*. Dublin, 1994.

Lyons, F. S. L. *Ireland since the Famine*. London, 1971.
————. *Charles Stewart Parnell*. London, 1977.

Mac Airt, S. & Mac Niocaill, G. (eds.). *Annála Uladh*. Dublin, 1983.

McCann, E. *War and an Irish Town*. London, 1974.

MacDermot, F. *Theobald Wolfe Tone*. London, 1939.

MacDonagh, O. *The Hereditary Bondsman*. London, 1988.

Macintyre, A. *The Liberator*. London, 1965.

MacManus, F. (ed.).*The Years of the Great Test*. Cork, 1967.

Mac Niocaill, G. *Ireland before the Vikings*. Dublin, 1972.

Mallory, J. P. and McNeill, T. E. *The Archaeology of Ulster*. Belfast, 1991.

Manning, M. *The Blueshirts*. Dublin, 1971.

Miller, D. *Queen's Rebels: Ulster Loyalism in Historical Perspective*. Dublin, 1978.

Moody, T. W. *The Londonderry Plantation 1609–1641*. Belfast, 1939.

Moody, T. W. and Martin, F. X. (eds.). *The Course of Irish History*. Cork, 1994.

Murphy, D. *Derry, Donegal and Modern Ulster 1790–1921*. Derry, 1981.

O'Brien, C. C. *Parnell and his Party*. Oxford, 1967.

Ó Broin, A. *Beyond the Black Pig's Dyke*. Cork, 1995.

O'Connor, F. *In Search of a State*. Belfast, 1993.

O'Faolain, S. *King of the Beggars*. London, 1938.

——————. *The Great O'Neill*. London, 1942.

——————. *The Irish*. London, 1947.

Ó Gráda, C. *Great Irish Famine*. Cambridge, 1995.

Patterson, H. *Class Conflict and Sectarianism; The Protestant Working Class and the Belfast Labour Movement 1868–1920*. Belfast, 1980.

Póirtéir, C. (ed.). *The Great Irish Famine*. Cork, 1995.

Raftery, J. et al. *The Celts*. Cork, 1964.

Ranelagh, J. O'B. *A Short History of Ireland*. Cambridge, 1994.

Roche, R. *The Norman Invasion of Ireland*. Dublin, 1970.

Roebuck, P. (ed.). *Plantation to Partition*. Belfast, 1981.

Rumpf, E. and Hepburn, A. C. *Nationalism and Socialism in Twentieth-Century Ireland*. Liverpool, 1977.

Ryan, D. *The Fenian Chief*. Dublin, 1967.

Saorstát Éireann, The Irish Free State, Official Handbook. Dublin, 1932.

Senior, H. *Orangeism in Ireland and Britain 1795–1836*. London, 1960.

Simms, J. G. . *The Siege of Derry*. Dublin, 1966.

——————. *Jacobite Ireland 1685–1691*. London, 1969.

Stewart, A. T. Q. *The Ulster Crisis*. London, 1967.

——————. *The Narrow Ground, Aspects of Ulster 1609–1969*. London, 1977.

Thornley, D. A. *Isaac Butt and Home Rule*. London, 1964.

Townshend, C. *Political Violence in Ireland: Government and Resistance since 1848*. Oxford, 1983.

Walker, B. *Ulster Politics: The Formative Years 1869–86*. Belfast 1989.

Wall, M. *The Penal Laws, 1961–1760*. Dundalk, 1961.

Walsh, J. R. and Bradley, T. *A History of the Irish Church 400–700*. Dublin, 1991.

Whyte, J. *Church and State in Modern Ireland 1923–1979*. London, 1980.

Woodham-Smith, Cecil. *The Great Hunger*. London, 1962.

Young, A. *A Tour of Ireland 1776–1779*. London, 1892.

INDEX